MW01520334

"I resonated deeply with the impacts in Diane's story as many of them mirror my own. As leaders, we are often told that giving to others is our greatest contribution, and while that is absolutely true, we can't give in healthy ways until we first give to ourselves. I strongly believe that recognizing and healing the beliefs formed from our early life experiences is our most important role as humans. This book provides a framework and tools to help readers do just that so they can show up as the leaders they were meant to be, contributing their powerful gifts to the world."

Tracy Maxwell, author of *Being Single, with Cancer: A Solo Survivor's Guide to Life, Love, Health, and Happiness*

ELEVATE POTENTIAL

A Conscious Approach To
SUCCESS

DIANE TAYLOR

THE
SELF
PUBLISHING
AGENCY

Diane Taylor
Elevate Potential — *A Conscious Approach To Success*

Copyright © 2024 by Diane Taylor
First Edition

Hardcover ISBN 978-1-0689430-3-4
Softcover ISBN 978-1-0689430-0-3
eBook ISBN 978-1-0689430-2-7
Audiobook ISBN 978-1-0689430-1-0

This book contains general information relating to various health and wellbeing strategies and corresponding transformational exercises. Such information is provided as a guide and is not meant to substitute for advice provided by a doctor or other qualified health care professional. The information contained herein is not for the purposes of diagnosing a health challenge or disease. You should always consult with a doctor or other health care professional for medical advice or information about diagnosis and treatment.

Book Design | Petya Tsankova
Editor | Andrea Greene
Publishing Management | TSPA The Self Publishing Agency, Inc.

for Ally & Matt,
my why;
my everything.

Contents

PART ONE

The Truth About Success

Introduction

"This is your life. Reclaim it."

Michael A. *Singer*

When you think about who you really want to be, what you want to achieve, and how you want to serve, what comes to mind? Are you on the path, taking steps to move towards that dream each and every day? Or is life looking more like an exercise in simply getting by and trying to find contentment? A large percentage of people are living what I call the zombie life. They wake up feeling tired, get ready for work, clock their 8–12-hour day, commute home, grab a convenient and often unhealthy meal, collapse exhausted on the couch while watching some TV, and then head to bed, where they lie awake ruminating over the stressful things in their life until they finally fall asleep. Then the alarm sounds, and it all begins again.

We have become an undernourished, sleep-deprived, stressed-out society embroiled in a mental health crisis. We are informed by the media, health care and Big Pharma. Why? Because these and other influential industries fund political campaigns. We have unconsciously given our power away to the institutions we are led to trust; in reality, however, their agenda revolves around their own power rather than the success and wellness of each one of us.

Obviously, you have already decided that you want more because you have picked up this book. You are ready, and I am here to help you create the strong, stable foundation to take your career and your life to the next level. Take a moment and celebrate your desire and your commitment to be the very best version of yourself. You are here because you are primed, and you are capable. I am honoured to be a part of your journey and to offer you some guidance and support in reaching your highest potential.

You are ready to fully embrace an intentional life and to start moving towards your goals and dreams in an empowered way. When you reclaim your authority and accountability and step fully into your true birthright as a leader, great things begin to happen. You will start to feel more aligned and will rediscover a sense of vitality and wonder that may have been elusive for a while.

If you are hesitating and thinking, *This sounds great, but I'm just not sure I can do this,* or *I really hope I can do this, but if I am being realistic, it sounds a bit out there,* then trust that you are precisely where you need to be. Being sceptical is a normal part of the growth process. If you continue reading and fully engage in the recommended reflections and transformational experiences outlined in Part Three of this book, you will begin to notice changes in how you show up and how the world reflects back to you. You will notice shifts in your confidence, happiness, success, and abundance. What do you have to lose?

Although I do not have a magic pill to offer you, you will experience no negative side effects when you show up for yourself and do the work. One thing I know for sure is that when we commit to ourselves, things begin to change significantly and in very positive ways. How do I know? Not only have I witnessed many of my clients experiencing positive changes, but I have also been doing the work and committing to myself for a long time now. Every time I show up for myself and commit to my growth and evolution, positive things happen. If I had had a book like this to refer to twenty years ago, I know I would have saved countless hours and endured much less struggle, worry, and stress. I want your life and the success you desire to be much easier for you. That is precisely why I wrote this book — so that you have immediate access to what took me decades to learn, often the hard way.

In addition to feeling slightly sceptical, it's natural to experience self-doubt and fear. You wouldn't be truly human if you didn't have some level of hesitation. This is your ego trying to protect you. You can instruct your "monkey-mind thoughts" to step aside because you are ready to experience a much better, happier, healthier, and more successful life. This will help release your fears and allow you to step more confidently into new ideas and practices that will level you up in the next chapter of your life. You are safe. In fact, you will be outstanding! Also, know that within the resistance, there are often keys to unlocking your true and highest potential. When you come up against something uncomfortable, stay curious and try your best to be open. Ask yourself, *Why am I feeling this way?* It might take some time for the answers to come but trust they will.

Do your dreams feel out of reach?

I have had the honour and privilege of working with many incredible existing and emerging leaders. As a Human Resources Professional and Consultant, I am often at the table when organizational and promotional decisions are being made. I collaborate with leaders at all levels to help them grow. I provide the best approaches for addressing people challenges and the most effective ways to align their people to their business objectives. This track record, combined with my own life experience, has provided me with deep insights into what can stand in the way of one's desire to be successful or to achieve the outcomes they hope for in their lives.

The biggest thing I have discovered is that people typically do not understand what is really holding them back from creating the success, wealth, and the relationships they desire. Most often people believe they are not experiencing success because of a lack of time, education, letters behind their name, generational wealth, or of being the wrong gender; these are all external factors, some of which they have no control over.

> *My client "Andrea" believed that if she could just complete her MBA, she would receive the elusive promotion she wanted so badly. Imagine her disappointment when that didn't happen. The good news is that this disappointment led to her to the real reason she was not advancing in her career. Fast forward — Andrea is now in the role she coveted and feeling much more satisfied with life; she'll be the first to admit that it was not because she received her MBA.*

We all set goals and try our best to achieve outcomes. When we fall short, we push forward and look endlessly for solutions — that one certification or a meeting with a key stakeholder, a course, diet pill, dating app, or podcast that will quickly and easily change everything. We look outside ourselves for roadblocks. We point fingers at things beyond our control, like the glass ceiling, where we come from, or the patriarchy, to name a few. It's easier to attribute our lack of success away from ourselves than it is to take full accountability and step into true empowerment.

But here is the secret.

It is only when we turn inwards and increase our level of self-awareness that our outside world begins to reflect back the goodness we long for. It's easy to blame other people or other elements. I would like you to do something for me now. Hold up your hand and point your finger. Do you see that there are three other fingers pointing back at you? You are the most powerful when it comes to having everything you are craving in your life; your fingers are directing you back to yourself.

And now for some context …

When I think back on my own life, much of it feels like a struggle, spent in fear and self-doubt.

Although my life has been truly blessed, how I got here certainly was not easy. However, for this too, I am grateful. I have learned many lessons and grown in incredible ways. I believe my own struggles are part of my purpose; without having truly experienced everything in my life, I could not empathize and connect with you on your journey towards realizing your true and full potential.

My experience has allowed me to be of service to many beautiful humans throughout my career. The gifts of struggle, pain, and grief have led me to a practice of self-work. This work affords me a deep and intuitive insight into meeting people precisely where they are at and providing them support and solutions to advance their own careers and personal lives.

You are a leader whether you lead a team of people or not! Each of us is responsible for leading ourselves. Although we are not responsible for what has happened to us in the past, we **are** responsible for overcoming our past and healing from it. Each and every day we have a choice — be a victim of our circumstance or become the victor of our lives. Success happens when we choose the latter.

Leaders choose victory. You are a leader!

You are not alone in what you are experiencing and feeling. In today's world, we are bombarded with social media images of perfectly curated lives, but these do not represent the full truth for anyone. Every human being is struggling with something. Many choose not to share as they feel shame or sadness about their experience. But here's the exciting part. Within you lies some pretty powerful and magical stuff. In the pages ahead, we will uncover more of your truly incredible potential and prepare you for your next level of success and happiness. You **know** that next level is there. The fact that you can already imagine it means that you are ready to go after it, and I am right here to support you in getting there.

Will it always be easy? Of course not. That is not how life is supposed to be. But is it worthwhile and totally achievable? Absolutely!

I promise to go deep and be truly vulnerable with you by sharing experiences that are not always easy or pretty. There are thousands of leadership books out there, and most focus on theory, scientific research, mindset, and best practices. However, I believe you picked this book up because you wanted something different, something more personally transformational.

I want you to walk away from this book and feel like it was an experience, rather than just a read, one from which you saw meaningful growth and change.

In the pages ahead, I will not only share my story of going from surviving to thriving, but I will also provide you with solutions and an invitation to go deeper. In Part Three, I will walk you through several different exercises that will allow you to personally apply the learnings to yourself. I want you to realize how unconscious patterns can impact our success and happiness in life; you may see similar story lines or impacts playing out in your life, even though your path may be quite different from mine. I encourage you to take your time as you work through the reflections since I believe that "the space in between" is critical for processing information and emotions. After all, this is your life — it is a work of art, not merely a task on your list of things to do.

Success is your birthright, and this book is the map. Ready? Yes, you are — let's do this!

CHAPTER 1

My Story

"When we share our stories,
we are reminded of the humanity in each other."
Michelle Obama

I was born into a happy middle-class family as a surprise second child, arriving only fourteen months after my sister. My parents had struggled to conceive Laurie, so much so that my mother was forced to quit her job. She wanted to be a mother more than anything, so her sacrifice to leave a career she had trained for ultimately produced the deeply desired outcome, a baby. My sister Laurie was born. Imagine her surprise when five months into motherhood, Mom learned that I was on the way.

My mother's strongest memory of being pregnant with me was how she thought I was going to be a boy. She wasn't excited to be a boy mom; she cried all the way to the hospital, thinking "Douglas Allan" was arriving that day, only to be overjoyed when I turned out to be a girl.

Life was typical for the first three years of my life. I had a loving stay-at-home mother and a father that was working hard to provide the best for us. I was a shy child whose older sister was pretty much the boss of me. For my astrology people, Laurie was an Aries, the most bold, focused, and confident of the cardinal signs— a leader. She did all the speaking, planning, and directing while I was happy to follow in her shadow and act as her side kick. I felt very content, loved, and safe in my place as the second born.

But, when I was three years old, life began to change quickly. In the fall, my sister became ill. After many doctor's appointments and my mother's insistence at getting to the bottom of the issue, Laurie was ultimately diagnosed with cancer that December.

She was the first child in Canada to undergo radiation treatment and chemotherapy at the same time. Although my childhood memories are spotty, I remember visiting her at the hospital and having to leave her room while the doctors attended to her. I can remember hearing her crying from down the hall. This memory still feels like a punch to the gut and brings a tight feeling in my chest and tears to my eyes. This is one of my earliest experiences of feeling and taking on other people's pain. To this day, I have a fear of needles, and being in a hospital causes me a high degree of anxiety.

Laurie passed away only four months later, on April 27, 1974, just two months shy of my fourth birthday. My experience on this planet forever changed that day.

The world I knew and felt safe in was turned upside down. Not only did I lose my sister, my very best friend, and my soulmate, but I lost the emotional presence and comfort of my parents who so rightly needed to withdraw in severe grief as they endured the most tragic of human experiences, that of losing a child.

There I was. My four-year-old self. Alone.

Today, we more deeply comprehend how the wounds we experience in our formative years are foundational. My personal experience is a textbook case. I have spent my entire life being fiercely challenged as I heal my core abandonment wound and all of the life impacts that accompany it.

In 1974, when my sister passed away, there was no real understanding about these impacts, nor were there any mental health-care resources. Neither I nor my parents had any form of counselling or professional support. My parents "soldiered on", and I was thought of as too young to be affected by my sister's death. But, in hindsight, it is crystal clear now that this loss and not having a space to process it has significantly impacted how I relate to the world around me.

The first time I remember being impacted by my unprocessed grief was in Grade 5. I was sick a lot. Looking back, I believe I was suffering from depression. I just didn't want to go to school. I wanted to stay home where I felt safe. My mom took me for many doctor's appointments and tests, but the results were inconclusive. One day, as I was sitting up on the exam table in a room at the Children's Hospital, the doctor came in and said to me, "You know, Diane, just because your sister died doesn't mean you are going to die, too." I was a bit shocked. I had never thought that! Or, at least, I had never **consciously** thought that. I was simply feeling sad and alone, craving some nurturing and safety, so I needed to stay at home to get that.

At the age of seventeen, in my senior year of high school, I was keen to start going out to bars and night clubs. I thought if I could only find Laurie's birth certificate, it would be the perfect

ID (the legal drinking age was eighteen in Alberta, and Laurie would have been eighteen that year). So, I went searching. I did not find the birth certificate; instead, I found a red binder filled with sympathy cards. As I read through the cards, my world started to implode, and the years of grief that had been tucked away came flooding in like a typhoon, drowning me in sorrow.

Over the next few months, I tried to commit suicide three times — the first two times by overdosing and the third time by slitting my wrists with a razor blade. As I sat on the floor in the back of my closet with blood gushing down my arms, I felt no physical pain, for the pain in my heart was so overwhelming I could barely breathe.

The scars on my wrists today are a constant reminder that if I do not do the work, heal the wounds, and process the emotions, the result will be bad. So, I show up and commit to myself each and every day, by working through the guilt for putting my parents through the fear of losing another child. What an incredibly selfish act! Seventeen-year-old me had no understanding of this. All I could feel at that time was my own pain, a pain that I desperately wanted to escape from.

After the three suicide attempts and putting my parents through hell, it was recommended I begin counselling since I was not going to improve without some form of intervention. And so began my lifelong healing journey.

Although your story may be very different from mine, I am certain there are elements that resonate with you because you too have experienced pain and sadness. In the next chapter, I will share how my story impacted the way I showed up which ultimately presented me with many challenges to overcome.

CHAPTER 2

The Impact of
the Formative Years

*"Trauma is not what happened to you, but what happens inside
you as a result of what happened to you."*
Gabor Maté

The formative years are from birth to age eight. During this time
frame, we experience the most growth cognitively, socially,
emotionally, and physically. These critical years have a signifi-
cant impact on how we navigate in our lives — I guess it comes
as no surprise that my experience losing Laurie in my formative
years has greatly affected my life. I have spent much time and
effort healing my behaviours and triggers in order to create not
only a stable but a successful life. There is always more work
to do, but I can say that I have grown and become much more
conscious. What I find exciting is that I can draw a direct link
between the healing growth in my conscious awareness and
my increased success both personally and professionally.

What follows are various impacts from my childhood experi-
ence that I have uncovered and worked on healing. These had
previously manifested as pain points that led me to behave in
overly emotional, controlling, unproductive, and unappealing
ways which, in turn, led to poor choices and outcomes. Gaining

awareness has been the path to empowerment and success for me. I trust my own experience will resonate with you, even if your formative years were different than mine.

Survivor's Guilt

I have spent an entire lifetime trying to convince the world, and more importantly myself, that I am worthy of a full and beautiful life, even though Laurie did not get to have that experience. I have heard that survivor's guilt is common when dealing with a loss. It is similar to questioning one's own self-worth. Have you ever thought to yourself, *Am I good enough? Smart enough? Tall enough? Thin enough? Strong enough? Fast enough? Pretty or handsome enough? Do I really have what it takes?* Perhaps you have thought, *Maybe I am just not cut out for this or who am I to think I can do this?*

We never receive inspiration to do or have something that we are not able to create. Once inspiration strikes, then fear and doubt start to creep in. I have asked myself questions like the above repeatedly throughout my life — *Am I worthy?*

Survivor's guilt kicks in and says, "Diane, you better pull yourself together and prove you are worthy!" Despite feeling like an impostor, I double down on striving for success since I am the one that got to live, and Laurie did not. I had better show up and be "good enough".

In high school, I was a member of every club, the VP of the Student Union, and a head cheerleader. In university, I was elected to student government, represented my school in an exchange group, and served as president of my women's fraternity. In my corporate career, I climbed the ladder in several male-dominated industries and was recognized as leader in my field. I have long been on a mission of excellence because anything less would signify that I am taking my spot here on earth for granted.

How does this affect my success?

Although I have an excellent résumé, there have also been some negative side effects in how I am viewed by others. I have been perceived as being intimidating at times. My high standard of achievement does not always inspire a similar performance in others. I can come across as being too direct, harsh, and unrealistic without having first gained the trust of others. When I am in a balanced, safe, and conscious space, I show up in a more relaxed, supportive, and even playful way that is aligned with my true being. I am a much more effective leader in this space.

Control Issues

When Laurie was dying, I could not save her nor control the events that transpired in the ensuing months and years. But when she was alive, I didn't require any control. I had a mother, a father, and an older sister that made things happen for me. I played the role of the baby, and life was great. I was happy, cared for, and adored. Things changed quickly as Laurie became sicker; I went from being in my happy bubble to being a very worried three-and-a-half-year-old who had to tag along to her medical appointments and visit her in hospital.

One day, as we were rushing into one of Laurie's doctor's appointments, we came across a dead bird on the sidewalk. My mom remembers this as a very upsetting experience. A few years ago, in a childhood regression therapy session, this event came up for me. It was in this session that I first realized that I couldn't do anything to alleviate my mom's desperation and worry about Laurie's situation or to change the direction of my sister's cancer. I had had my first glimpse of not being in control.

Then Laurie passed away, and I was alone. I had lost my sister, my best friend, and my champion. My parents were overcome with grief. There was absolutely nothing I could do to control the circumstances, and I felt powerless. I felt like the rug had been pulled right out from under me; in the space of five months, my world and who I was in that world had turned upside down.

I never wanted to experience something similar again. So, I became a control freak. Some may even say I have mild OCD tendencies. But really, who doesn't want all the coffee cup handles in the cupboard facing the same way? If my world is in order and I can control my direction and ensure positive outcomes in my life, then I will be safe. The human behaviour theory of "the only thing worse than bad is uncertainty" resonates deeply with me. Rather than seeing a range of beautiful possibilities in the uncertainty, I am transported back to the place where I lost my footing, and I do not feel safe.

How does this affect my success?

I have self-sabotaged several times in my life by choosing bad over uncertainty; I was not able to control the space of uncertainty and guarantee my safety. I became burnt out and exhausted trying to force outcomes.

In the many psychometric tests I have completed over the years, there is a common theme. The results are usually split right down the middle between high-performing and high-supporting components. If I were to analyse this, I would say that the highly supportive, relaxed, and playful part of me is my true being. The high-performing driven components are survival instincts resulting from the core wounds sustained in my formative years.

Suffering in Silence and Feeling like a Burden

As a child and even a teenager, whenever someone would say the word "cancer", I distinctly remember feeling like I had been sucker-punched in the stomach. A burning sensation would form behind my nostrils, and tears would immediately well up in my eyes. Many times, I would find an excuse to escape to my room and cry with my head under a pillow so no one could hear. I was afraid that if I cried in front of my mom and dad, it would awaken their pain and suffering, and they would once again emotionally withdraw. To this day, I still struggle when sharing any sadness or suffering, even with my friends. Somewhere in the depths of my psyche is a girl who believes that sharing will burden others and push them away.

For most of my life, I have felt a sense of guilt for having any emotional needs of my own. I have always assumed the role of supporter and nurturer of others. But when I felt sad or could have benefited from the support of another, I typically withdrew for fear of being needy. This behaviour sends a signal that says, "I am not of value. My needs do not matter."

But the game-changing truth is that until we can value ourselves by understanding and appreciating our needs, attracting what we need, whether it be success, money, or love, will be a challenge.

I have a long history of blocking my own abundance because I believed that being a strong, independent woman who is emotionally balanced and not one of those "needy women" was the right way. Clearly, I am not the only one who thinks this way because I often see memes on social media that fuel this type of thinking, things like, "No one is stronger than a person who never asks anyone for anything." If you have ever felt empowered by such a statement, then you are among a large group of people, me included, who need to heal the wound that created this toxic belief; quite frankly, it is holding us back from everything we deserve.

It is possible to be confident and independent while still needing the support of others from time to time. Allowing yourself to receive this support without viewing yourself as a burden is a natural, healthy state of being. You are valuable because you are participating in the reciprocal process of giving and receiving and not because you give until it hurts.

Spending your life being of service to others while blocking the natural flow of receiving will eventually lead to some level of resentment. The need to be loved and supported is an essential human need. When we push aside our needs and soldier on, we cast a dark shadow on what we need to thrive.

How does this affect my success?

Although I would like to be of service in the image of someone beautiful and full of light like Mother Teresa, that is not always the part of me that shows up. If I do not allow my own needs to be met, it makes it much easier for my unconscious triggers and resulting behaviours to emerge. **She** is the intimidating version of me who exhibits a sense of superiority and is agitated when others are not seeing her vision. When **she** shows up, all the good work I have done is forgotten because her negative energy suffocates any good intentions.

When I honour my needs and ensure that I am taking care of myself and intentionally creating balance, **she** is set free, and my true, kind, supportive, and highly influential self can take up more space and achieve more success.

Fear of Deep Intimacy

One of the biggest impacts of losing a core connection in my formative years has been the belief that deep, soul-connected love will result in loss or abandonment. I have been in a lifelong pursuit of trying to match the connection I had with my sister, one in which I feel adored and cared for. My healing journey has allowed me to better understand how I have adapted as a result; I push away deep love connections to protect myself from abandonment.

How does this affect my success?

We attract what we put out there energetically. I traditionally attract men who are also experiencing fear on some level, whether consciously or unconsciously. They have either a fear of fully committing to a real and deeply connected partnership or of losing that life-long partnership; this suffocates any true potential for a healthy relationship. Although my conscious being wants more than anything to be in a loving, supportive relationship with a man who will make me feel protected, my unconscious beliefs have produced a debilitating fear that has prevented this from happening, protecting me from another life-changing loss and a lifetime of sadness and pain.

Perhaps you have heard the saying "what we believe we achieve"? This has played out for me on repeat. My best friend in grade school moved to Australia shortly after we graduated from high school. My best friend in university moved to Norway. And my lifelong best friend fell in love with an amazing American and moved to Texas. Most people would view this as the natural evolution of life; however, I see it as a continuation of my "abandonment story".

As I become more conscious and work on changing this deeply rooted core belief, I now consider my best friend moving to Texas as a blessing that has allowed me to change my story. Although she is in a different country, she has never abandoned me. Our support and love for each other is as constant and unwavering as ever.

The Veil of Disconnection

A veil of disconnection is an unconscious protection response. When painful events happen in our formative years, they impact our behaviours and life experiences without us really understanding and or even being aware of it.

Over the past few years, I have decoded my experience with my birthday. Birthdays are meant to be happy celebrations of the beautiful soul that you are. However, I have always felt awkward on my birthday and, to be completely honest, just sad. Not sad that the years are passing me by or that I am getting older. Just sad — not wanting to be the centre of attention and having no real understanding of why. Sure, I appreciate all of the birthday love and attention my beautiful friends and family always shower on me, but even that doesn't take away the sadness.

Things became clearer after doing some childhood regression work with a skilled professional. I'm not going to lie — the work was hard. I felt completely emotionally exhausted after each of the two sessions I did. But there were some significant positive outcomes and healing, and I now understand why my birthday makes me sad.

In the sessions, the practitioner initially took me through a hypnosis-inducing protocol. Then she asked me to go back to the first memories of my childhood. I discovered experiences that created imprints around me not being able to control outcomes, to make sure everyone was happy, or to please my parents which might cause them to withdraw their love.

After one of the "Let's take you back to another memory" prompts, a birthday party came into focus. It was my fourth birthday, and I was at the head of the table in my family home, a homemade cake my mom had specially decorated in front of me, squiggly, coloured balloons overhead, and friends from the neighbourhood all around me. But in between me and this experience was a translucent, grey-coloured veil separating me from the celebration. I was disconnected from the emotions of joy and adoration. Rather than being the centre of attention, I was alone on the other side of the veil.

How does this affect my success?

The veil of grey, I now understand, was grief. My fourth birthday occurred only two months after Laurie passed away. I experienced something similar when my father passed away. I distinctly remember feeling this veil or sense of separation, like I was one step removed from reality. My theory is that this is a natural coping mechanism when we are grieving. We are removed one level to be able to cope with the first-level feelings of loss. If we were fully present, the loss would be too much to bear, so we adjust in order to survive the initial stage of the grieving process.

The imprint of my fourth birthday party impacted my future birthdays until the childhood regression work moved the memory into my conscious mind and allowed it to be healed. I may never have been able to release the subconscious imprint and have a different, more fulfilling experience without it. Since then, I have celebrated a few birthdays, and they did feel very different. Although I still downplay it, the special people in my life make me feel celebrated and connected on my special day.

My hope is that reading about the impact of my formative years has brought some of your own life experiences to the surface, even though they may be different. We all have unresolved ramifications from our experiences. Most of the time, we have no idea how these affect how we behave, show up, and experience life. Some can create positive behaviours that lead to our success and purpose in life. Others that stem from our unconscious and unhealed experiences lead to less than desirable feelings, behaviours, and outcomes that do not fully support our desires.

Consciousness is defined as the quality or state of being aware, especially of something within oneself. Only 5% of what we experience in our lives is informed by our conscious minds, and the remaining 95% is informed by our subconscious mind. We can increase our level of consciousness by healing the wounds created through our formative year experiences. When you do this, your ability to naturally attract the success and happiness you desire also increases.

You may have had several experiences in your life that are unaddressed because you found them too painful, you were never taught how to process emotion, or you are unaware of the negative impacts of unprocessed emotion. So, you simply soldier on. You may feel overwhelmed, exhausted, or anxious. The dreams, desires, hopes, and wishes are still present. They just feel slightly out of reach, like you are missing a road map to help you get there.

Well, I have some exciting news! This book is my best attempt at providing you with a road map to elevate your consciousness, to let go, and to heal that which is holding you back. My deepest desire is for you to take back your divine power to achieve your highest potential and to create your most successful, happy life, the one you have dreamed of and truly deserve.

But before we do that, let's look at how elevating your level of consciousness can affect your ability as a leader by focusing on the unconscious versus the conscious leader.

CHAPTER 3
The Unconscious Leader

"You don't lead by hitting people over the head — that's assault,
not leadership."
Dwight D. Eisenhower

If you think back on your career for a moment, I am guessing you can identify at least one or more supervisors or managers that were less than fabulous. Or maybe you've reported to some really nice people who were lacking the capacity or qualities to actually lead. They may have had titles that deemed them leaders or they may have been above you on the organizational chart, but their responses or behaviours have rendered them ineffective.

In my own experience both in the corporate world as a leader and in my current work coaching and developing leaders, I find that most people have good intentions and want to be successful leaders. They may have many exceptional qualities and often a great deal of knowledge and experience. However, certain behaviours cause a lack of buy-in or an inability to garner trust from the people they lead. This disconnect impedes their true potential and desired success in their professional and personal lives.

We are starting here because it is always much easier to see flaws in others than it is to shift the focus inwards and to inventory ourselves. Think about the supervisors and managers you have either worked with or reported to. Are there ones that stand out as being frustrating, demotivating, or downright mean?

Several years ago, I had the opportunity to work with a consulting company whose Human Resources Manager had just resigned. A former colleague, a good, trustworthy guy, reached out and asked if I was available to take on a new client, a CEO named "Greg". In our first meeting, I met a no-fuss, "let's get to it" kind of man. As I am results oriented, I can appreciate a direct approach. However, as the weeks passed, "no fuss" Greg quickly became a cranky, unbearable human that was not happy with anything I produced, recommended, or presented. This was a new and very different response for me; most of my clients are very grateful and highly value my work. For a short time, I bought into his style, trying my very best to please him by working faster and harder. I believed that something was wrong with me, despite hearing from many other employees that they felt as stressed out and anxious in their workplace as I did. After a few weeks, it became evident that I did not have the power to influence him. I did my best to look inwards and see if there was anything I could change in my approach; I quickly learned that no matter how I shifted, turning this business relationship into something positive and productive was not going to happen. Greg felt that he was a more intelligent person who knew better than anyone on his team, me included. At that point I knew that even though I could have really used the income, the stress and anxiety of dealing with Greg was not worth it, and I chose to part ways. I'm not sure I have ever come across a less conscious leader over the years. Greg definitely wins the prize.

Fortunately, the lion's share of people I have had the opportunity to work with over the years have been perfectly competent leaders. But, that said, there is usually one or two factors that hold them back from being exceptional leaders. Alternatively, some leaders excel in their work life but cannot seem to achieve the happiness they yearn for in their personal lives.

When we look at what holds us back, 95% of the time it is something in our subconscious. Remember that only 5% of our day-to-day experience is informed by our conscious mind. This is a natural and normal human experience; understanding and learning how to tap into and grow that 5% is the ultimate success hack that will produce the life we all deeply crave.

Your Shadow Self

Each of us comes into this life as a whole and perfect being. Then life happens. We experience challenges or traumas that significantly impact us. These challenges create core wounds, and we form stories around these core wounds. We go through life being triggered and having uncomfortable experiences and emotions without understanding why. Since 95% of our experience is operated by our subconscious mind which in turn influences our actions and feelings, it's no wonder life can feel so complicated at times. This in turn can lead to a feeling of helplessness.

Helplessness can easily make you to feel like a victim of life's circumstances. The victim mentality is a feeling that life is happening to you. In addition, often when we experience challenging things and feel like it's us against the world, the people around us will respond in a supportive way. We no longer feel alone. This can lead to an unhealthy subconscious pattern of purposely creating chaos in our lives in order to get that next hit of kindness and feeling of connection.

How does this play out in terms of unconscious leadership?

When we have unprocessed core wounds, they can cause unconscious triggered responses that are less than desirable. Carl Yung was the first to describe this as our shadow side. Shadow refers to those parts of us that we cannot fully see or understand because they have not been brought fully into our conscious awareness. Think about walking down the street on a sunny day. In front of you on the sidewalk, you see your shadow. It is a dark and fuzzy reflection of yourself, unlike what you would see if you looked in a mirror. It stretches out in front of you, even larger than your real physical being. Your shadow side is not dissimilar to this.

I have witnessed various common unconscious behaviours or shadow side themes in my work, and I have personally experienced several of these myself. Some I have managed to heal and overcome, but others still occasionally appear when I am not in full balance. As you read through the shadow side behaviours that can hold people back, you will recognize people in your career and life who fit these descriptions. You might even recognize yourself! Notice if you feel resistance; it might very well be a clue that this is one of your own subconscious shadow side behaviours.

The Dreamer

These managers are usually fun, supportive, and inspirational. They excel at brainstorming. They love to collect ideas, theories, and knowledge and to read a lot of career-related books. They love to tell you how many books they have read, and they feel their value increases with that number. They frequently share ideas on what they are currently reading. However, they struggle at executing or implementing any of these great ideas they learn about. When they report in at the next meeting, very little, if any, progress has been made.

The Executor

The opposite of the Dreamer is the Executor. The Executor gets shit done. They consistently deliver on time and on budget. If a team member needs a deadline to be extended, they get frustrated and feel extremely anxious. They need to control and drive outcomes in order to feel happy and successful.

The Educated

Having the right credentials is foundational; however, the Educated feels that the more letters they have behind their name means the more worthy they are. They believe that it is primarily their education that drives their success. They often struggle with core requirements like executing on their commitments or developing positive and supportive relationships with peers and colleagues. They believe that the letters behind their name are what generate influence rather than their results and outcomes.

The Martyr

The Martyr needs to be needed. They project in a subtle (or sometimes not so subtle) way that the company would be lost, go out of business, or flounder without them. If you ask them, they will say that they work harder and are more committed than anyone else. They can feel threatened by other high-potential colleagues and will share disparaging comments about them with their supervisors; taking them down ensures they can remain in the perceived Number One spot. The Martyr clicks on the memes that say "No one is stronger than a person who never asked anyone for help". They are driven by their need to be significant and are typically too busy to train others, something that might decrease their own significance.

The Warrior

The Warrior prides themself on being strong, competent, and fierce. They accomplish things through intimidation and use fear to motivate people rather than cooperation. In meetings, if someone offers an alternative opinion, they may interrupt and speak louder to maintain a level of control.

The Toxic Positive

Positivity is a critical element in being a strong leader. However, so is being realistic and accepting the duality in life, that there is light and dark in all situations. The Toxic Positive person only presents the positive and sends the vibe that they are "holier than thou" or unable to truly connect as their veil of perfection separates them from others. Either way, this quality generally comes across as insincere and decreases the ability to create trust and connection.

The Controller

This shadow side runs deep for me, and I continually have to work on being aware of when it emerges; I must take a step back and gain a new perspective. The Controller is not a "go with the flow", "hope outcomes happen" type of person. They feel unsafe when things are unclear or undefined, so they push, force, and overengineer. Their behaviours are driven by the fear that at any given time, the solid ground they stand on will crumble, and their project, goal, or life in general will fall to pieces. In order to manage their anxiety, the Controller keeps a firm grip on schedules and action items, and when things are not tracking as precisely outlined, they become frustrated, cranky, and difficult to work with.

The Afraid of Conflict

Life is full of conflict, and, in most cases, that is not a bad thing. Different viewpoints or opinions lead to innovation, continuous growth, and improvement. That being said, it is quite surprising how many people suffer from a fear of conflict. It's likely that all of us do to some degree. The Afraid of Conflict plays out the worst-case scenario in their mind which leads to avoidance. They do not expect rational conversations in which two parties calmly share differing approaches to come to a consensus; rather, they envision heightened and uncomfortable emotions. They simply "turtle" and agree with what others present to avoid any potential conflict, instead of having a voice and possibly contributing in a meaningful way.

The Perfectionist

The Perfectionist really struggles in moving projects ahead or completing tasks in a timely manner because they do not feel comfortable until they are perfect. They hold themselves to such a high degree of excellence that whenever they make a mistake or receive constructive feedback, it pains them deeply.

For The Perfectionist, "good" is often perceived as "not good enough"; often, opportunities will pass them by as they fail to act or deliver on time.

The Narcissist

The Narcissist always knows best — just ask them. They believe they are the most intelligent, best-suited, and most strategic human in any arena they appear. They often have many other shadow sides described here that combine into an impenetrable state of being. This is a very toxic state, one that cannot simply be coached to change. Narcissists possess wounds that are so significantly deep that there is little room for self-awareness or a willingness for growth and development.

These common behaviours weave throughout our lives as we typically have no awareness of where they stem from or how to soften their impact. Let's face it — it's easier to avoid growing, evolving, and becoming better versions of ourselves. It's easier to point the finger at external factors, getting caught up in repeating patterns and experiencing more pain. It's easier to avoid working on the most important thing we need to create a peaceful, happy, and abundant life ...

Ourselves.
Our self-awareness.
Our consciousness.

But clearly, you are committed to growth. You are here now reading this book which means you are already ahead of the curve, and you are ready to take your success even further. You have probably been working on your growth and development for some time now. You know that on the other side of your personal struggles and pain is something called victory. You have made the choice to overcome your challenges, heal from your wounds, and be the champion you were meant to be.

Because you are a leader!

A true leader is aware of their behaviours and of how others perceive them. They notice when they are triggered by their emotions in a negative or unproductive way and seek to gain understanding, grow in self-awareness, and heal so they can show up in their highest form, in their true potential.

Once you step into this phase, life magically starts changing; there is more ease, and things start to effortlessly flow towards you without you having to push, pull, or persuade the hell out of them.

This is called consciousness. Rather than blaming external factors, you look inwards and ask, "How can I change my thoughts, feelings, or actions to get a different result?" Mindvalley, the world's most powerful life transformation platform, indicates that only 30% of people are in a state of consciousness while 70% of people are stuck, believing life is happening to them, rather than for them.

When we expand our consciousness and understand that life is happening for us not to us, we understand that even the most challenging and heartbreaking life occurrences happen for a reason. We will somehow grow and become better versions of ourselves as we navigate each experience life has to offer us.

CHAPTER 4
The Conscious Leader

*"Conscious leadership is the art of leading with both the heart
and the mind, fostering a mindful approach to inspire
and empower those we lead."*
Folusu Gbadamosi

Now that we have a good understanding of how unconscious patterns affect how we show up as imperfect humans and sometimes less than desirable leaders, let's shift our focus to where we are headed — becoming the very best versions of ourselves as healed, conscious leaders. It is in this state of being that we have the ability to create and attract everything we desire.

Simply defined, a conscious human is a person that believes that life is happening for them, not to them. They know that even life's most difficult challenges, struggles, and traumas are part of the journey of human experience.

Let me tell you the story of my most favourite boss ever, Brian.

Early in my career, and shortly after starting as a management trainee for a car rental company, I was fortunate enough to be selected from several applicants to become the group's first Human Resources Professional. This marked the beginning of my career in HR. I loved my work, but after my divorce, I was really looking for a change in my life. I was growing tired of the prairie winters and longed to be close to the ocean. An opportunity to apply for a position in Vancouver arose, and after receiving my current boss's approval, I applied. Off to Vancouver I flew for my interview where I met Brian, the GM of the British Columbia group. I was hired!

Brian was highly charismatic, positive, fun, strategic, and capable, but there was more. About a month after moving to Vancouver, it was Thanksgiving time. Brian knew I was not going home to see my family as I had just relocated. At this point, I had met my brand-new colleagues and only one other person in the city. Brian and his wife were kind enough to invite me to their home to celebrate the holiday with their family. At this point, I was fairly inexperienced in my career; I was still learning, making mistakes, and definitely suffering from some unconscious leadership behaviours like the Perfectionist, the Executor, and the Controller. There had been more than one occasion where I ended up crying in Brian's office. However, despite how green I was, despite my imperfections, I always felt like Brian supported me, had my back, and most importantly, believed in me. He provided clear expectations and showed me how to win; when I did win, he high-fived me! I always felt like he was a champion for the company, for me, and for my career. After two years, I left the company as my daughter had been born and the long commute and hours were no longer compatible with my life. To this day, however, I keep in touch with Brian on occasion.

Brian is a great leader, but if you were to talk with him, I am confident he would share stories about some of the challenging, unconscious behaviours in his own journey; after all, he is human. Despite these challenges and personal triggers, he is committed to always being the best version of himself for his team and his family.

Once we reach a personal level of growth and join the 30% of people who are conscious — the people who understand that life is happening for us, not to us — we can springboard to becoming servant leaders. Rather than just showing up each day in survival mode, we are able to be present for those around us, to serve beyond ourselves.

When we arrive at this place, we see certain qualities or positive behaviours that start to shine through. When working with conscious leaders, the following are the qualities I have seen that seem to stand out.

The Developer

The less-than-conscious leader can feel threatened or insecure at times. They fear that if someone has more knowledge or expertise than them, they might be replaced. As a result, they do their best to keep people in their place, not sharing new information or encouraging them to grow. The conscious leader understands that when you develop the people around you, your job gets much easier and more efficient; you are actually recognized as a great leader. Conscious leaders care about the people they lead and intentionally support their career growth. They understand that when a co-worker is not growing, they will not feel engaged and may choose to move on, leading them back to square one — recruiting and training a new person. This not only causes them more work but also increased costs to the company. Unconscious managers are afraid that if they invest in and develop their people, they will leave. Sometimes this does in fact happen because retaining employees forever is not realistic. However, people who feel held back in their careers are significantly more likely to look for new opportunities outside of the company and will leave earlier than those who are evolving.

The conscious leader is a Developer, working with their direct reports as well as people in all areas of the organization to intentionally plan for growth and development. They understand the risks in not developing their employees and conversely recognize the value in doing so.

The Visionary

If you do not know where you are going, how will you ever get there? Whether you are currently in a leadership role, or if you are simply leading yourself, a clear vision of where you want to go is critical to your success. The Visionary knows where they want to be or what they want things to look and feel like in the future. In order to create your vision, you must first intentionally pause. Step off the hamster wheel of life and dream for a few moments — imagine a future desired state. Once you have clarified your desires and created your vision, you can then proceed to developing goals that will get you there. We will work on this together in Part Three.

Conscious leaders understand that this is a powerful process that allows them to intentionally move towards their goals, dreams, and desired outcomes despite all the challenges life never fails to present. Painting a vivid picture of the future creates a solid, inspired direction for you to focus on even when obstacles appear. When leading other people, conscious leaders share their vision often and include their team in achieving this vision.

The Communicator

Have you ever heard a manager say, "I told them that already" or "That's just common sense." These are words uttered from an unconscious place. Communication is one of the most powerful tools we have to create understanding and alignment, and yet most people struggle with effective communication. Common communication challenges include:

- avoiding speaking up or sharing thoughts or opinions
- listening to respond rather than to understand
- not listening at all
- communicating to appear intelligent rather than to gain understanding
- talking to just be heard or to control the conversation

I'm sure you have been on the receiving end of these unconscious communication patterns. Additionally, you would not be human if you didn't engage in some of them yourself. Being aware of them can help you grow.

The conscious leader understands how powerful communication is and that people can sometimes fall back into unconscious communication methods. However, they intentionally strive to improve upon their effective communication skills. They know that communicating something once does not mean it was heard or understood by everyone; humans, although trying their best, are often distracted or unfocused when coping with life's hidden challenges.

They understand that repetition is the key to learning. Building a layered communication plan around key messages is critical to progressing with ease.

They understand that there is no such thing as common sense. In order for there to be common sense, there needs to be common experience. Each human is divinely unique (just like their fingerprint or eyeball scan) and presents with unique experiences, formative year wounds and triggers, impressions, and current challenges. Conscious leaders are in tune with these realities and lead from an understanding and appreciation of them.

The Provider of Recognition

Have you ever heard a manager say, "They get a pay cheque — why do I need to recognize them?" I have unfortunately heard this a time or two over the years. Although it is not technically a requirement of management to recognize employees or for you to recognize the important people in your personal life, why wouldn't you? The conscious leader understands that a simple act of recognition or a thank you goes a long way. They know that feeling appreciated makes people feel good and that they will want to repeat whatever actions they are being recognized for.

As young children learning how to behave in our homes and the greater world around us, our parents recognize and celebrate the behaviours they are teaching us so that we will repeat them. Think about the formative year experience every single human goes through — potty training. When I was training my children, if they went on the potty, they got an M&M and a sticker for the sticker chart, and then we all sang and danced around to the potty song.

Similar experiences in the first years of life create connections in our brain that inform how we are motivated and perform for the remainder of our lives. From the ritual of potty training, it is evident that what is recognized is repeated.

Sometimes, when I mention recognition, the hesitation I encounter is around budgetary concerns. However, there is a distinction between recognition and reward. Recognition costs little to nothing. Although it is nice to have rewards, if they come without recognition, they do not hold the same influence over continued positive behaviour.

The conscious leader knows that genuine positive feedback is a powerful way to engage and motivate people so they will continue to strive to do their best. The unconscious leader worries about how the recognition will be received because their ego mind is always vigilantly protecting them. Conscious leaders make a point of finding outcomes to genuinely recognize each week so that it becomes a habit and part of their conscious leadership behaviour.

The Empathetic

At a minimum, we spend half of our waking hours at work with our colleagues. Conscious leaders are fully aware that behind every employee performing a specific role to achieve a specific outcome is a human being experiencing life. Everyone is dealing with "stuff" outside of work. Having a leader who knows who we are outside of work, what is important to us, and who supports us when we are having life challenges can actually create a space where we can perform better. Many times, I have seen people that are experiencing challenges step up and perform because they genuinely appreciate the care their leader has for them. It is no secret that we will perform at a higher level for those we respect and who care for us as people, not just employees. Conscious leaders who regularly schedule one-on-one check-in meetings, not only for project status and goals but also for the well-being of the human sitting across the desk from them, naturally tend to have more productive and engaged teams.

The Celebrator

In the introduction, I talked about "the zombie life". It is so easy to get stuck in a pattern of survival repetition, to just keep plodding along. We know this is what leads to exhaustion, overwhelm, and depression. When we focus on what's next on our list of things to do, we can get stuck on what I picture as "the hamster wheel of life". The conscious leader understands the power of defining, catching, and celebrating **wins**.

Imagine for a moment that you are writing an email to a friend and do not use any punctuation. The words just merge together endlessly — no commas and no periods. It would be hard for your friend to comprehend what you are trying to communicate. It would be impossible to read and decipher the email, and in the end, what you intended to communicate may not even come across well. Without pauses, end points, wrap-ups, or celebrations, life can feel indistinguishable. This leads to burn out and a decrease in productivity.

Conscious leaders understand that including "punctuation" in the work schedule and flow of work can positively impact people's energy and motivation. They are very aware that they cannot get more hours in each day, so they consider how they can optimize their own energy and that of their team instead.

Conscious leaders communicate their vision; they show each team member their role in helping the team achieve that vision, and they create rest stops and celebrations along the way. They understand the pride and positive energy that is created when people are on a winning team. When the team is not winning, they find smaller things to celebrate until the little wins create momentum for even bigger wins.

The Coachable

Conscious leaders understand that in life we are either growing or dying — just like a plant. They know they are human, and therefore, have flaws and behaviours that are less than enlightened. They commit to their growth and learning by reading, working with coaches, therapists, or mentors to identify pitfalls, work through challenges, and expand their way of responding to and approaching people and situations in new and more effective ways.

The Board of Directors

Conscious leaders surround themselves with what I refer to as a "Board of Directors". Obviously, some leaders have a literal Board of Directors; however, what I am referring to is a group of people that make them efficient, effective, and therefore more successful. These people are often subject matter experts or designated in certain skills or talents. Unlike the unconscious leader, who believes they have to do everything themselves to be valued, the conscious leader knows that when they surround themselves with area experts, they will become more successful. I have never met a person that excels in every function or skill. Each of us has a unique set of talents that give us much more leverage. Trying to do everything means utilizing valuable time struggling through work that does not fall under one of your superpowers. Although they can figure out most things, it takes much more time. Not only can this decrease your level of efficiency, but it can also feel exhausting.

The conscious leader finds people who have superpowers they do not and adds them to their "Board of Directors"; relying on others is not a weakness but a strength.

The Unity Seeker

Everywhere you look there is a "fight" or a division. Humans spend a great deal of time and energy asserting and affirming their own opinions and beliefs. Being right has become our primary focus rather than finding win-win solutions to advance outcomes for all.

So why do we need to be "right" or "win"? It's simple. It validates our self-worth. However, conscious leaders have a higher degree of self-worth, so rather than trying to validate themselves, they can more easily collaborate and be open to new ideas.

If we were to consider how much of our lives we spend trying to force outcomes, I'm guessing it would be quite high. Yet, one of the natural laws of the universe clearly indicates that what we resist will only persist. What would it look like if we stepped out of the battle long enough to observe ourselves, our intentions, and actions and shifted to a different mindset?

Conscious leaders seek to understand beyond their own ideas or opinions to find the best solution for all stakeholders rather than to simply assert their dominance or superiority because they are deemed the leader.

By now, you likely understand that we are all a work in progress. I am confident that you resonate with many of the qualities of a conscious leader, but I am also fairly confident that because you are a human being, there may be some unconscious patterns or triggers that surface. I know for me personally that is the case. You wouldn't be reading this book if you were not on the path to becoming a more conscious leader. Understand that not all days will go well; you will still struggle and be triggered by old subconscious patterns. The more aware you become, the more prepared you are to grow. Remember in these times that you are perfectly human and refrain from beating yourself up for not being fully enlightened. Be kind and supportive to yourself like you would with a friend. Acknowledge yourself for your awareness, give yourself a pat on the back, and create an intention to understand and release whatever no longer serves. Your growth is going to lead to incredible things.

PART TWO

You Are the Answer

CHAPTER 5
Establishing Balance

"Balance is not something you find, it's something you create."
Jana Kingsford

We have all been led to believe that true fulfilment and success evades us due to external factors. After all, it's much easier to point fingers than to consider the ones pointing back at us when we do. The glass ceiling, your gender, your education, your race, the economy — you name it, there are countless external factors we can easily attach blame to if we want to stay stuck.

But that's not you. You are stronger than that. You know you can create the life you have always dreamed of, but you just need to know how. Since you were never given a roadmap or taught these approaches in school, how would you know?

You now know the way to skyrocket your success is to increase your consciousness. To be in that top 30% of people who understand that life is happening for them, not to them. You now possess this knowledge. But you also understand that 95% of your experience is being informed by your unconscious mind. So how do you move towards a higher level of consciousness?

You create balance. You heal. You take your power back.

In this section, we are going to talk about why balance is such an elusive concept and how to redefine our understanding of it before moving on. In Part Three, I will teach you some transformative practices to advance healing both the conscious and unconscious parts of you that will in turn help you move forward with the confidence, grace, and high-vibrational energy that attracts success. I am excited to share these ideas and practices with you because I have no doubt they are going to be game-changing for you.

Excited? Let's go!

Pain

Pain is a naturally occurring part of life that we do everything in our power to avoid. Avoiding unprocessed emotions means avoiding pain. It's a survival instinct. We run, and meanwhile, these emotions lie dormant causing us to feel unhappy, unfulfilled, or on edge. This, in turn, may cause us to numb ourselves with unhealthy addictions. We turn to our escape of choice — comfort food, alcohol, drugs, sex, pornography, retail therapy, extreme exercise, or simply creating chaos in our lives.

The problem is that when we do not process and release our pain, it starts to corrupt our cells just like a computer virus. A computer virus greatly impacts the performance and workability of your computer, just like unresolved emotional pain can create disease in your body and impact the way you show up and respond to situations.

Louise Hay was a pioneer in discovering which emotions or negative thoughts create different diseases in our bodies. Her book *Heal Your Life* is truly revolutionary. In fact, whenever I feel any ailment coming on, I immediately turn to this book for clues on what might be happening emotionally to allow the disease to pass through.

2012 was a very difficult year for me. It began with my father passing away in January. Losing my hero, my protector, and my leadership mentor was enough to deal with, but the year continued to serve up more challenges. At the time, I was still working in the corporate world for one of Canada's largest retail brands. While I was away for my father's passing, I received an important meeting request for the morning of my first day back. The meeting was to discuss several project starts that year that would involve mass lay-offs in my region. I proceeded to coordinate and facilitate the closure of five big-box locations and relocate functions for five support departments to another province. Once that was complete, I had to reduce my team by half. During the process, I was in champion mode. Planning and executing, ensuring everyone was treated with respect and dignity, marching forward while laying off thousands of people — affecting the lives of thousands of people! Every night, I tossed and turned as I was unable to sleep on my left side. There was so much pain along my ribs! I now clearly understand the emotional-physical connection. My ribs on the left side of my body were protecting my heart, a heart that was aching from having to deliver bad news to so many people.

I am here to support you with a different approach that will help you truly uncover what is holding you back. Not only will you increase your level of conscious awareness and process emotions that may be hindering the happy, successful, and fulfilling career and life you are craving, but you will also naturally become more physically healthy as a result.

Let's begin with you. All of you. The whole you.

Balance

Achieving a work-life balance seems to be an impossible feat in today's reality. We all wear many hats in our lives, and it can seem like the idea of finding balance is a pipe dream. However, when we are in a state of balance, we are able to show up much differently than when we are not. The balanced state allows space for an increase in consciousness and the energy we emit into the world. The more balanced we are, the higher our energetic frequency becomes which leads to an ability to easily attract more of what we desire.

Obstacles to Balance

There are three significant obstacles to balance: the model we use, our propensity to look outside of ourselves, and our lack of wholeness.

Obstacle # 1 - The Model

When we think about balance, we think of the work-life balance model where one half of our life is work and the other half is life. This idea places work and life in opposition to each other like two opposing sports teams on either side of the field. When there are two opposing forces, only one can take home the win. In the work-life balance model, inevitably one part will triumph as we struggle to find balance.

When we shift to what I prefer to call the Relationship Balance Model, we can more easily create balance in our whole lives. If you place yourself in the centre of this model, you will discover you have many relationships. You have a relationship with your work, your partner, your children, your friends, your community, and most importantly, yourself. This model nourishes all of our high-priority relationships and reframes work as one relationship among many in our lives rather than as an opposing force.

Obstacle # 2 – Looking for Answers Externally

I don't know about you, but I am a sucker for Instagram advertisements that offer me the next health breakthrough. I have a cupboard full of supplements, some of which I take daily and others (which I ordered looking for a quick fix) that proved to have no results. It would be amazing if we could just find that one magic pill that made all of our challenges, health obstacles, and pain go away. We spend so much time seeking answers outside of us, whether as a supplement, advice from a trusted friend, or the latest podcast we listen to. But each time we lean outside of ourselves, we tilt a little bit more towards a state of imbalance.

The more we learn to go within to find solutions, the more balance we create. The right answer for what you should do, even down to what supplement will support you the best, always lies within. The challenge is to replace seeking answers externally with turning in and listening. This is an excellent practice for developing a balanced state of being.

Obstacle # 3 - A Lack of Wholeness

As a human being, you are the sum of your physical, mental, emotional, and spiritual parts. You have a body, brain, heart, and spirit. North Americans tend to suffer the most in trying to find balance in our lives; we are uber-focused on only two realms, the physical and the mental. Imagine if you woke up in the morning, ready to drive to work, but two of the four tires on your car were flat. You wouldn't get very far, would you? And yet, we wonder why we feel off balance. In the next chapter, we will take a much closer look at you from a whole-being per-spective.

Curious? Read on!

CHAPTER 6

You Are a Whole Being

"Seek to be whole, not perfect."
Oprah Winfrey

Let's take a deeper look into the four realms and how they interact with each other to create a balanced state of wellness. Without this understanding, it is very easy to leave parts of ourselves unnurtured; this imbalance negatively affects us in many different ways from our health and physical well-being to the way we show up, how we are perceived by others, and ultimately how we create success.

The Physical Realm

When we talk about wellness, people automatically think about our physical wellness. We are always chasing the latest health trend or the newest, hottest workout regime. It's not surprising considering the economic impact. In the US alone, sales of supplements are expected to reach $77 billion by 2028. Despite significant growth in all things related to physical wellness, disease and obesity rates in North America continue to grow significantly every year. A lack of understanding of the full picture of wellness combined with the zombie lives we have adopted leaves us desiring a quick fix or magic pill. It makes sense then that sales of supplements, magical concoctions, and pharmaceutical drugs continue to rise.

Don't get me wrong — our physical health is foundational to our ability to lead full, happy, and successful lives. Anyone who has ever experienced an illness understands that without our health, we have nothing. However, when we understand how the other parts of our being (mind, heart, and spirit) interact and affect our physical wellness and ultimately our success in life, we can then empower ourselves to proactively take care of our whole selves rather than just our bodies.

Our governments and health-care systems do not want us to take authority for our own wellness. If we are healthy and have strong immune systems, there will be significantly less disease, and private health care and Big Pharma will thus not receive the enormous profits they currently do. Governments fund their over-the-top, lengthy, and expensive election campaigns from donations made by companies and industries that benefit from us being sick; it would not serve them well to actually get to the root of the issue by empowering and educating us on how to be healthy and well.

Imagine for a moment a beautiful day in the future where we have learned how to actually heal ourselves and be well. A world where there was significantly less cancer, diabetes, depression, or obesity. Where medical schools spend more time educating our doctors on how nutrition impacts inflammation in our bodies — the root cause of most disease. This would have a significant negative impact on our economy.

In the summer of 2022, I woke up one morning, the right-hand side of my body frozen. It was both scary and painful. I wasn't sure what was actually going on. Was I having a stroke? As the day went on and I moved around more, I started to gain more mobility. But I also had a significant rash on the side of my leg.

I Googled my symptoms. My search led me to discover that I am in the 2% of people in the world who have an allergy to cobalt. The rash on the side of my leg could be linked to a Vitamin B12 allergy (B12 has the same molecular structure as cobalt).

About a month prior, I had gone to a naturopath to see why I was not able to lose weight. I was eating protein, veggies, and healthy fats and was walking and meditating daily, yet the scale wouldn't budge. He believed the issue to be stress related — that my cortisol levels were preventing my body from releasing the weight. He recommended I do several Stress Buster Vitamin Cocktails via intravenous. Although I wasn't sure I was that stressed, as I was meditating every day and life was actually quite peaceful, I trusted the medical professional and agreed to it. To provide some perspective, one intravenous cocktail has the equivalent of ten vitamin B12 injections. In hindsight, after the first session, I felt extremely depleted and had to go to bed at 7:00 p.m. It wasn't until the second intravenous session, when I had the equivalent of twenty vitamin B12 shots in a two-week period, when my body shut down and screamed loudly, "You'd better figure this out!" And I did.

I started to piece the evidence together. Twenty years prior, I had had some allergy testing done and was provided with a list of foods I had intolerances for. Oatmeal was high on the list; I later found out that oatmeal has a high nickel content. I now understand that the other items on my intolerance list were also high in nickel. Although only 2% of people in the world have a cobalt allergy, 15% of women have a nickel allergy. Interesting to note: these two elements are side by side on the Periodic Table. I continued to do more research and took an online course on Systematic Nickel Allergy Syndrome. I discovered the signs and symptoms had always been there. I get a rash on my belly from the button *on my jeans. I don't have pierced ears because I used to get itchy, flaky, and bleeding skin from wearing earrings. I have suffered from similar-looking rashes at different times in my life which I can now link back to getting B12 injections. I got those B12 shots because I was always tired and couldn't lose weight. However, they simply exacerbated the issue. The inflammation in my body from eating food high in nickel and injecting cobalt via vitamin B12 was keeping me tired and fat. The sad thing is that many people who have a nickel allergy are unaware of it, and the inflammation in their bodies from eating healthy foods that are actually high in nickel results in secondary diseases like obesity and many autoimmune disorders (the body's histamine levels are increased by constantly trying to save them from the allergy).*

My takeaway from all of this?

What is deemed healthy may not be for everyone. Although kale, avocados, nuts and seeds, fish and seafood, oatmeal, whole grains, and coconut are known as the cornerstone of a balanced diet, they all happen to be also high in nickel. Knowing what foods do not work for me may not have helped me reach my ideal goal weight, but I look significantly thinner because I am much less puffy from inflammation.

Another takeaway is that even the most highly trained, excellent physicians and naturopaths cannot know everything. I would never have expected them to diagnose my cobalt allergy or to even be aware of it since it affects only 2% of people in the world. There is very little research on Symptomatic Nickel Allergy Syndrome in North America. Fortunately, I was able to find some research from Italy as well as a nurse in Florida, Kristina David, who has a very helpful online course. Our health and well-being are our responsibility.

We need to become a partner in our health care rather than simply relying on our team of medical professionals to provide direction and advice.

The Mental Realm

The mental realm is the part of you that functions from your mind. It encompasses your ability to think, plan, and execute your goals. It is the realm that separates humans from other species. The mental realm is where our positive and self-limiting thoughts happen. It is also where the ego resides — that little voice inside us that typically tries its best to keep us small and playing safe. It is the home of knowledge.

We live in a world that places a high degree of value on knowledge when it comes to success, whether it be the information we collect or our educational accolades. One of the highly complimentary phrases we assign to people we respect and want to emulate is that of a "thought leader". Knowledge is indeed a very powerful thing if applied to achieve effective results. However, I have also seen how it can disempower people. To look at knowledge, university degrees, or designations as the pinnacle of success is not the most conscious application, and I can advise you with complete certainty that they will not solely result in success.

I have had numerous conversations with some exceptionally brilliant and successful people (many of whom have no higher education or designations) who have at one time or another felt inferior because they did not have additional letters behind their names. In fact, my own father, my most admired leadership mentor, only completed Grade 8 prior to lighting the world on fire.

Often when emerging leaders are trying to advance their careers, they believe they have to pursue more education or get an advanced degree. Now, clearly, there are some industries and several career paths that require certain minimum educational requirements; I am certainly not saying that advancing your education is a bad idea.

What I am saying is this — having an advanced education will not guarantee success in your career or your life, nor does it make you more worthy. So, before investing a lot of time and money in further education, take some time to really dig deep and ask yourself, *Why do I want to pursue this degree or designation? Is it a requirement for achieving my career goals, or will it add more joy to my life because I love learning?* Make a conscious choice rather than unconsciously trying to fill a void of self-worth; I guarantee that if you are feeling unworthy because you do not have a certain degree, getting one will not change that.

Many years ago, I hosted a gathering of women at my home for a celebration. I noticed one guest reference her master's degree within moments of being introduced to several different people. This is certainly not the first time I have witnessed someone enumerating their educational qualifications in an attempt to assert themselves as a highly educated, intelligent person. I have also seen people insert subtle references to their advanced degrees in social conversation. This may signify that the person may not feel worthy which is certainly not true. Of course, there are also many highly educated people who do not do this. This is the conscious space where they value their education but also know that it is just a small piece of their worth and what they have to contribute. If someone has an unhealed wound that is manifesting in a lack of self-worth, no amount of education is going to heal that wound — just ask my client "Andrea" whom

*I spoke of earlier. A deeper look into the other realms and estab-
lishing balance will be where the elevation occurs.*

I have seen many people with MBAs, master's degrees, or even
PhDs not get the job or the promotion. Even if education is a re-
quirement, it is only one facet of the desired qualifications; al-
though the candidate may have a great deal of knowledge, they
may be lacking in other critical elements of leadership, such as
modelling positive behaviours, meeting deadlines, being orga-
nized and executing plans, doing what they say they will do,
and promoting the team before themselves. Don't forget emo-
tional intelligence aspects like building trust and gaining buy-
in. Let's face it — just because you have specific qualifications
or you know how to do your job well does not mean people will
trust, respect, or follow you. These are key elements of being
a leader.

When we focus too much on one realm without incorporating
input from the others, the results are often disappointing as we
find ourselves out of balance and unable to show up the way we
need to in order to become successful.

The Emotional Realm

The emotional realm or heart space is where our feelings re-
side. This realm greatly informs our thoughts (mental realm)
and has an impact on our bodies (physical realm). When we ex-
perience low-vibration feelings like fear, grief, shame, or guilt,
the energy they emit has a negative impact on our well-being
and what we are able to achieve. When we experience high-
vibration emotions like joy, courage, or love, these emotions
have a positive effect on our well-being and open us up to at-
tracting abundance.

In dealing with my formative year trauma and the ensuing grief and depression, as well as not being in favour of most pharmaceutical approaches, I have had to learn alternatives. Creating balance in my emotional realm by learning how to maintain a positive, high-vibration state has been a game changer in my ability to show up confidently and to generate successful outcomes.

I can remember in my late teen years and early twenties doing the exact opposite. I would sit around playing dramatic, dark music and wallow in my sadness. Now I know if I am feeling sad that I need to be intentional in shifting my energy rather than being swallowed up by the negative vortex. For me, that means talking through things with my best friend, going in nature and taking a walk at the beach, playing some upbeat music and dancing to shake off the negativity, and feeding myself high-nutrient foods, despite my cravings for macaroni and cheese and warm chocolate chip cookies; comfort foods will satisfy my current desire for warmth and sweetness in my life but will in no way help me feel better or allow my body to function optimally. Emotional eating is a great example of how our feelings can affect our physical and mental realms. Feeding your body comfort foods will leave you less mentally alert and lethargic.

Humans are not generally well-educated in feeling, processing, and healing our emotions. However, I do believe that every generation is improving. I come from the last generation (Generation X) that was to be "seen and not heard". If you laughed too loud, cried, or expressed your needs, you were immediately hushed and sent away. I come from a family who suffered a significant emotional trauma, losing a five-year-old child, and yet none of us received any counselling or grief support. We just swept the emotions under the rug and soldiered on; many years later all my unprocessed grief came bubbling up and erupted like a volcano.

For men, it was and still is much more difficult. Men are expected to be strong and show no signs of vulnerability, or they will be perceived of as weak. Men are told to "suck it up" and "be a man" which translates to maintaining a confident, unemotional stance. Have you ever seen a photograph of a men's sports team? They don't even smile. This diversity in the way women and men are encouraged or discouraged to display their emotions has created a divide, and workplace and personal relationships between men and women can be challenging as a result.

Unfortunately, we lack balance in our emotional realm because we lack an understanding of how to create it; we have been socialized to believe the strong thing to do is to avoid and carry on. This is where the danger begins. Without the wisdom to process and heal our emotions, we show up as beings that are out of balance and easily triggered, and as a result, unable to create the respect, trust, and buy-in leaders require to be successful. Unhealed emotions do not simply disappear. They are stored in our bodies and energy fields and can and will affect our cellular formation resulting in disease.

The Spiritual Realm

The spiritual realm is where your soul resides. It is where you connect with something bigger outside of yourself. This realm is likely the most difficult to understand because it holds all the things we cannot see.

It is where we hold our beliefs in a future reality that has not yet been achieved and all things that live outside of our current 3-D experience. Spirituality is not religion; however, many people practise or access their spirituality through their religion. Perhaps you believe in a powerful source outside of yourself, or you are an atheist that believes in nothing beyond our free will and the impact of our choices. No matter where your beliefs lie on this continuum, you have hopes and dreams for your future, things you want to make happen but may not be real yet. Think of this as the spiritual realm.

Another way to explain the spiritual realm is through what we call our gut instinct or intuition. Each of us has a sense of "knowing" that lives within us. It's uncommon to link this to the spiritual realm because religion has trained us to believe that Spirit or God, Allah, Buddha, the Universe, Source — whatever you call it, it lives outside of us. But the truth is, Spirit lies within each of us. We are divine beings created in the image of Spirit. If your religious practice strengthens your connection to Source, then that is awesome. Understand that you do not have to identify with any religious practice to experience the gifts and power of a divine source connection. It's not something you have to achieve or earn. It just is. It's in you, wherever you are, whether kneeling in a church or sitting at home. Wherever you go, there it is.

Your spirit or soul is the eternal part of you that lives on when your breath leaves your body. It is connected to something greater than your body, mind, or heart. This connection is where your intuition lives, that deep knowing within you, and also where your higher levels of inspiration come from. When connected in this realm, you can feel a much greater degree of peace and flow in your life. It is the divine truth from Source that calms and quiets the ego, that part of your brain or mental realm that feeds your low-level thoughts. When connected and balanced in this realm, your purpose lifts you up to overcome your limiting beliefs. If you make space and are open to intentionally connecting to this part of you, the guidance you seek comes to you as whispers of knowing and inspired thoughts.

In my own journey, the more I lean into this powerful part of me, the easier things become and the more aligned and positive I feel. As I continually grow my own spiritual practices, the more I feel connected to that deep, fulfilling love my soul has been seeking since my sister passed away. There is a knowing that I am not alone; even though I am a self-employed, single mom with a lot of responsibility, I am not alone. I know I am co-creating abundance and happiness with and through Source, and this provides not only a strong grounding but also the required inspiration to keep moving forward day by day, week by week, and year by year.

My own experience began with a connection to a magical and supportive spiritual dynamic beyond what I could see or touch in the physical realm early on. I started to connect to the spiritual world around the same time I was experiencing deep grief in my late teens. One day, I decided to go to the cemetery where my sister was buried. I don't remember going there when I was growing up. I didn't mention to my parents what I was doing or ask for directions to her gravesite because, again, I did not want to stir up their grief. So, I just went. As I drove into Queen's Park Cemetery, a 136-acre space of land with over 65,000 burial plots, I wasn't sure I would ever find my sister's grave. But, somehow, I felt led. I moved in a direction that felt familiar and right. I knew that Laurie had a flat grave marker, and I seemed to remember it being up on a hill where you could see houses across from the site. It didn't take very long at all until I found it. When I was at such a low point in my life, I needed that. The ease with which I found the site made me feel supported and connected to something bigger. As I sat beside her gravesite, feeling sad and uncomfortable, a rabbit appeared just off to the right. I immediately felt uplifted and happy at seeing this sweet, gentle animal interact with me. And so began "the signs".

I now practise daily meditation which creates an intentional space to connect to Source, that "something" outside myself. My daily practice provides me with the air I need to breathe. It feeds my soul. If you think about your spirit for a moment and what that is, it is your breath. The moment you take your last breath is the moment your spirit leaves your physical body. It is your breath that feeds your soul. When you connect to your breath through exercise, breath work, or meditation or experience moments that "take your breath away" (through high-vibration emotions like pride, awe, wonder, gratitude, and love), this is how you connect with and nurture your spirit, bringing yourself to a more complete state of balance and wholeness.

Where do you get your most inspired ideas or intuitive downloads? For me, prior to starting my daily meditation practice, I would get these intuitive hits when I was alone driving in my car or sitting at my mirror putting on make up — two things I do instinctively, without concentration, thought, or effort because they are automatic. Because I do not need to think to perform these tasks, they create a wide-open space in my mind. Is your experience similar? Do you instead practise your spiritual connection through your religion? Think about the rituals you perform effortlessly. Do you receive downloads when you work out or go for a walk? Several people have told me it happens when they ski — they are in flow with the wide-open expanse of snow and sky. The key is to discover where you experience these moments of connection, where inspired ideas or action steps flow to you naturally, and to create more opportunities to receive this divine guidance and momentum.

When we are disconnected from Source, we can easily get stuck in the "monkey mind" — thinking, rethinking, and overthinking — which increases our anxiety and causes two things to happen. First, we move forward in ineffective ways that often need to be changed or corrected, and second, we shut down in overwhelm and take no action. If you are someone who procrastinates, you may want to try increasing your connection with Source simply by feeding your soul; focus on your breath or on things that take your breath away and see if it helps.

When my connection to Source decreases because I get too busy to do the practices that feed my soul, I feel lonely. Despite being surrounded by incredible family members and amazing friends, I feel solitary, like I don't fit in or that I'm different from everyone else. Our societal conditioning of believing we have to be perfect through the curated half-truths portrayed in social media, separates us from our true worth and divine birthright of being perfect just how we are, in this exact moment.

When I feel unworthy, I move further away from my centre, and an imbalance happens. The more I compare myself to things that are not real, the more my self-worth suffers. This creates all kinds of disconnection, an inability to perform at a high level, and a general loneliness. All of us thrive when we experience a deep connection to something outside of ourselves. This is why I do everything in my power to ensure I perform my daily practices.

When we come home to the Source that literally lives and breathes within us, we regain our sense of being grounded and whole. When we connect to the spiritual realm (however we may get there), we are no longer alone. We step into a deep, peaceful, and life-affirming sense of being. In this space, inspiration flows naturally and freely. Stress and anxiety release, and our internal light increases and expands. This high-vibration frequency we emit attracts love and abundance. What we are is what we receive. When we tap into our truth, divine beauty, worth, and anything we desire can easily be ours. This space is within you and is yours to access. You just need to let go of the wounds, triggers, and societal conditioning that are holding you back from connecting to your true power and magic.

The Symphony of Wholeness

The physical and mental realms are foundational. Without our health, we have nothing. If we cannot think, we cannot plan or take action. However, focusing primarily on these two realms alone can create an imbalance. When that happens, life feels hard and out of alignment. There is a huge body of research that continues to grow daily on the interconnectedness of these four realms and how they interact.

We know our emotional state greatly impacts our physical state, but do we truly understand that when we are mentally or emotionally uneasy, our physical bodies respond to the state of "dis-ease" and our cells start to create physical disease within our bodies?

We tend to refer to and think of the realms as forming a pyramid with physical as the base, followed by mental, emotional, and spiritual at the peak; however, this pyramid flows both ways. Yes, we need our health (physical) as a basis to think and process information (mental) which allows us to feel things (emotional) and connect to our purpose and direction in life (spiritual). But it also works in reverse. As we take our power back and become more conscious (spiritual), we heal our emotional wounds and triggers (emotional), gain more clarity of mind (mental), and our nervous system relaxes and creates equilibrium in our bodies (physical).

When we expand beyond the physical and mental to a whole being encompassing the physical, mental, emotional, and spiritual, we naturally move to a balanced state of well-being. This balanced state is where we can begin to develop and elevate our consciousness. This is where we move beyond knowledge and embrace wisdom. Wisdom is far more powerful than knowledge as it is a combination of knowledge and experience. It is within wisdom and balance where you will easily create the successful life you know you deserve.

CHAPTER 7

You Are Energy

"Everything is energy."
Albert Einstein

Before we dive into this chapter, I want to remind you that you are the answer. When you change that which is in you, that which is around you also changes. It's so easy to get caught up in looking for direction and answers outside of ourselves, in believing we do not have everything we aspire to because of external factors. In so doing, we actually give our power away. However, when we fully understand that life is always happening for us, we take our power back, elevating our self-awareness and ultimately our consciousness. Life becomes a whole lot easier; the things we long for, whether in our careers or our personal lives, start to appear effortlessly.

You are an energetic being and, as such, emit an energetic charge out into the world around you. That charge can greatly fluctuate based on how you feel. The higher the vibration you emit, the more success and abundance you will attract.

Let me tell you about "Grace". She really wants to have a successful career and personal life, but she is such a negative, "glass half empty", "poor me" kind of person. I remember one time she told me, "I tried manifesting, and it didn't work so I gave up.

That is just bullshit anyway." Oh, Grace! What she is missing when it comes to positively manifesting her desires is energy. Grace clearly stated her desires and then emitted the energy levels associated with not having what she wanted, rather than trusting that it was already on its way to her. Her low-level vibration was so constricted that it prevented her desires from reaching her.

Scientists measure the energetic frequency of human emotions emitted in hertz (Hz). On a regular day, most of us are in the 200 Hz zone or just getting by. When we feel certain negative emotions like shame, guilt, fear, or grief, the energy we emit decreases significantly. We constrict and withdraw. The reverse effect happens when we feel positive emotions such as pride, acceptance, love, or joy. The energy we emit increases, and we enter an expanded state. Have you ever noticed a time in your life when things were going well, and everything seemed to come together? When things are good, they are really good. Or the opposite — when you are already feeling down and then another bad thing happens, you feel like you just can't catch a break. When we are in a contracted state, because we are emitting a low-energetic frequency, we are unable to receive abundance; however, when we are in an expanded energetic frequency, abundance in all forms is attracted to us with ease. You are basically like a magnet. The higher your frequency, the stronger your ability to attract all the good things you deserve into your life.

The illustration below, by David R. Hawkins, MD, PhD, developer of the Map of Consciousness and author of *Power vs. Force,* shows the different energetic frequencies emitted based on an emotion. In order to ensure you maintain a high-level vibration, it is imperative to process low-level emotions as these do not simply go away. Avoidance may remove the emotions from your daily thoughts; however, you now understand that your thoughts reside in the mental realm and that unprocessed low-level emotions remain in your energy field and have an impact on your life experience. Dr. Hawkins mentions that 99% of the world's population is living in a contracted state (below 200 Hz), causing them to suffer or just get by. The only way to release these emotions is to allow space for them, process them, and then let them go. In Part Three, we will work together to help you do this.

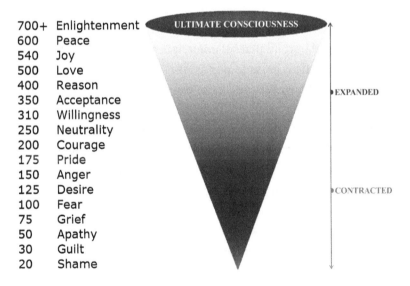

Emotional Vibration Frequency Analysis Chart
[Source – Blisspot.com]

When you understand how your emotions impact your energetic vibration, it is easier to commit to the work of increasing your vibration because you know how truly powerful it is. By processing the unhealed emotions that are creating a lower frequency, you cut the ties that are holding you back; you are now free to elevate to a more expanded state where you will attract everything your heart and soul desires from a place of ease and playfulness.

Have you ever had an experience where things were going really well for you, but something in the back of your mind wondered if it was too good to be true? Or has a niggling fear ever made you question if the rug could be pulled out from under you at any second? Our nervous system actually has a set point, a place where we feel comfortable and stable. As a result, when we expand beyond that set point, it is a common to feel unsafe and naturally regress to our smaller, less abundant set point. We have all heard stories about people who win the lottery and within just a few years are back to where they were before winning the lottery. This is a perfect example of how even though a significant expansion can create an opportunity, the nervous system set point will ensure that a contraction happens to maintain that safe, familiar feeling.

Another example of how our nervous system keeps us stuck in familiar places is of people who suffer from chaos. You know who I am talking about — they talk about wanting a peaceful life or relationship, but since they have never either experienced one nor witnessed peace in their formative years, their nervous system set point makes anything outside of what they have experienced feel unsafe. Chaos is their safe set point, the familiar. No matter what they say, they continue to attract and create chaotic or unstable situations and relationships in their lives.

When I think of chaos patterns, I can't help but think about "Madeline". When I was first introduced to her, she was looking for a new home as her father had just passed away, and she could no longer afford to live in his home. She had recently been let go from her position and was legally pursuing the company for wrongful dismissal. She said she was unable to work as she had to clean out the excessive hoarding from her dad's place, so money was extra tight. The week before she had planned to rent a truck and take a load of cast-offs to the dump, she broke her arm falling off a horse. Wherever Madeline looked, she seemed to find trouble. For some unconscious reason, Madeline was attracting chaos.

Our beliefs and stories form a foundation for the emotions we experience and the energy level we reside in. Our patterns will continue to play out until we truly heal the emotional wounds and triggers that are causing our nervous system to feel safe in that contracted state. Once we heal, we can expand and create a new identity.

The Chakras

Another way to understand yourself as an energetic being is through the chakra system. Chakras are the energy centres within and beyond your body. Chakra is a Sanskrit word that means "wheel". Chakras were first written about by the Vedas in India around 1500 – 500 BC. Although many yogic texts indicate that there are 88,000 chakras within your energy field, we commonly refer to seven main chakras as illustrated below:

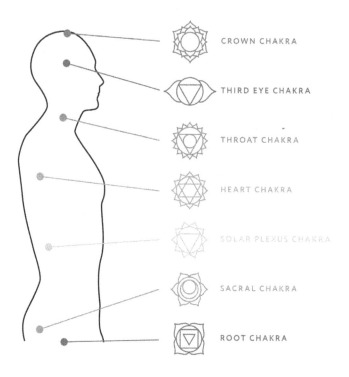

CROWN CHAKRA

THIRD EYE CHAKRA

THROAT CHAKRA

HEART CHAKRA

SOLAR PLEXUS CHAKRA

SACRAL CHAKRA

ROOT CHAKRA

Each one of the chakras emits energy that is either expanded, balanced, and in flow or constricted and stagnant. Our experiences and how we perceive them impact the energy our chakras emit, and this affects how we move forward and where we struggle to find ease. When we create balance in our chakras, we create a positive, high-vibration state that allows us to move more easily through life and attract the success that has previously eluded us.

Certain low-vibration emotions are linked to each of the chakras. Here is a list of the seven main chakras and the low-vibration emotions that will create an imbalance in each energy centre:

Root Chakra	(Red)	Fear
Sacral Chakra	(Orange)	Guilt
Solar Plexus Chakra	(Yellow)	Shame
Heart Chakra	(Green)	Grief
Throat Chakra	(Blue)	Lies
Third Eye Chakra	(Purple)	Illusion
Crown Chakra	(Golden White)	Attachment

Conscious leaders are grounded (balanced root chakra), creative and innovative (balanced sacral chakra), confident (balanced solar plexus chakra), caring (balanced heart chakra), able to communicate effectively (balanced throat chakra), capable of aligning their teams to their inspired vision (balanced third eye chakra) and feel like they are a part of something bigger (balanced crown chakra).

Conscious leaders understand that the power lies within. When we turn inwards and focus on creating balance, we show up very differently. We vibrate at a high frequency. Everything we imagine can become ours much more easily. In Part Three, we will investigate the chakras and learn more about how you can bring each of them into balance.

Yes, you are the answer to everything you dream of. Almost everything in the external world has no real or consequential impact and can be overcome when you turn your focus inwards and work on your most important asset, yourself.

So, come with me as we move into the next section of the book where I will walk you through some transformational experiences and exercises that will create a whole new experience for you. I'm so excited for you. You are a champion for committing to yourself. High five!

PART THREE

The Path to Lift Off

CHAPTER 8
A New Vision

"Where there is no vision, there is no hope."
George Washington

You are here because something inside you understands just how powerful you are. You now know that by bringing yourself into balance, elevating your levels of consciousness, and maintaining a high-vibrational energy, you will become more successful, happy, and fulfilled.

But first, let's address the elephant in the room. That sounds a little bit scary, doesn't it?

It is well known that often the thing that holds us back from success is not the fear of failure, but rather the fear of success. Here are some common unconscious beliefs that play out and prevent us from stepping into our true power:

- If I am successful, I will separate myself from my friends and family because they will be jealous or think I just want attention.
- If I am successful and earn a lot of money, people will think I am a diva that doesn't care about others, and I want people to know I am warm, caring, and understand what they are going through.

- If I am successful, it will take away from my spiritual essence and desire to help the less fortunate or those suffering in the world.

There are other beliefs that may be playing in your subconscious mind, attempting to protect you but ultimately holding you back.

In order to cut through the confusion and chaos in both your conscious awareness and your subconscious beliefs, it is important to create a new vision. This vision will help create focus and overcome the noise and overwhelm happening in your mind.

Most of the time we do not get to where we want to go simply because we aren't clear about where we are going.

Let's imagine for a moment that you are in a boat in the middle of the ocean, and you want to get somewhere. Right now, you are just floating, and the conditions change daily depending on the weather and time of day. You really hope to get to a better place, but you are unsure where that place is. One day, you paddle a little bit in one direction and do not reach somewhere better, so the next day, you row in a different direction. Other days, the wind and rain descend on you, and you just huddle up and row nowhere. Can you see how this boat analogy demonstrates what your life might look like when you do not have a clear vision?

In order to extricate yourself from this lack of direction and to arrive at a more comfortable, stable place, you need to make a plan. Sure, you could just start rowing and hope that you will reach a desirable destination, but you are brighter than that —

you know hope is not a strategy! Instead, you will vision, plan, and execute because you are a leader, and you have the ability to turn your dreams into reality.

Once you choose the destination — your vision — you can already start imagining being at this destination. This will remove you from the low-vibration feelings of fear, doubt, and confusion — floating aimlessly in the middle of the ocean in a rocking boat with the cold wind blowing through you. It will put you on solid ground and vibe you up. Imagine feeling the sand between your toes and the sun warming your back; you are being served delicious fruity drinks served in pineapples, you hear lively music playing, and you are surrounded by smiling people who are relaxed and having fun.

A vivid and visceral vision of what it will be like once you arrive at your destination will enable you to push through any obstacles you may encounter while rowing. If the winds get stronger, you will focus on the delicious sweetness of your pineapple drink and row harder. If the temperature drops, you will concentrate on the sun on your back, maintain your focus, and move forward. Visualization is one of the most effective tools in creating what you want.

Create Your Vision

The Oxford Dictionary defines "vision" as the ability to think about or plan the future with imagination or wisdom. Neville Goddard, the pioneer of visualization, stated that what is in your imagination will harden into reality. We imagine a future time and consider what we want to achieve. This is why establishing a clear vision will increase our successful outcomes.

Creating your vision and then being in the high vibration of your vision is the recipe for co-creating the life you really want. Let's do that together right now.

What do you want your life to look like one year from now? Understand that you can pick any future timeline, however, I recommend that it be no less than three months and no longer than five years. Write it down. Yes, you can certainly do this in your mind, but if you take the time to grab a piece of paper and a pen, you will create more clarity and cement your vision into reality more effectively. In fact, you might want to grab a special journal or booklet as you work through all of the exercises here in Part Three.

Think about it like this. You go out for dinner to a fantastic new restaurant in town. It is busy, and there is a lot of hustle and bustle. The server comes and takes your order. They are the type of server who prides themselves on not having to write anything down. You place your order, including any special dietary requests. By the time your server reaches the kitchen, they have stopped to serve other patrons with more water and takeout boxes. When they reach the kitchen, they do not remember the details of your order and have to come back to the table to ask for clarification. By the time you get your meal, you are hungry and cranky. Or worse, because they were embarrassed that they forgot the details of your special requests in your order, you eat the incorrect meal and end up suffering from a stomach ache.

If you simply think about your vision, without taking the time to commit it to paper, your outcome might not be as successful. Think about creating your vision as putting in an order to the universe. The more detailed you are about it, the better your outcome will be. Wishy-washy thoughts will only equal wishy-washy results. Be clear and be decisive.

With the future date that you chose in mind, think about these questions:

- Who do you want to be?
- What do you want your life to look like?
- What position do you want?
- What kind of leader do you want to be?

Next, you will want to review these important points:

- Why do I want this?
- Where am I right now?
- What do I need to do to achieve my vision?
- Are there any obstacles I may encounter along the way?
- If so, how will I overcome them?

And a final but very important part of the process:

- What will I feel like when I achieve my vision?
- How will I celebrate my accomplishment?
- What song will I hear playing?

Your Song

Athletes are known for having a pre-game song to pump them up and shake out their nervous energy. Music is powerful as it has the ability to immediately bypass your mind and take you right to your heart. Aligning a song with your vision will elevate you and help you move past any obstacles by increasing your energetic vibration. Your song acts like a hot-air balloon that lifts you up above the fray, realigns you with your vision, and keeps you moving forward. So, make sure your song is on your playlist and listen to it anytime you need to be elevated.

Aligning to Your Priorities and Values

In order to ensure you are not only achieving goals but also moving to a more fulfilled life, it is important to align your vision with your own personal values and priorities.

*Although it was never a personal goal to be recognized as a leader in Human Resources, I was very fortunate when one of my work teams nominated me for Human Resources Professional of the Year. Being selected as a finalist and having an opportunity to address my peers in a meeting celebrating the three finalists was an incredible opportunity and a day I will never forget. It is also an achievement that looks really good on my list of credentials. However, there was something very distinct about that day for me. After it was all over, there was a feeling of emptiness. The high from being recognized in such a grand way was not sustainable. That recognition was icing on the cake. But what **has** carried forward from that day and holds deep meaning for me is that my team, the people I was leading and serving every day, chose to nominate me. I had somehow inspired and cared enough for them as people that they wanted to take the time to go through the nomination process. Each member of this team is now shining bright and advancing their own HR careers in roles across many different industries and locations. Watching them continue to grow and thrive is one of the most rewarding experiences I have ever felt, and that is the part that is sustainable. When I see my clients, some with whom I have worked for almost a decade experiencing success, it completely lights me up. That is because this is aligned to my priority of serving others and my value of growth and development.*

Not quite sure what your real priorities are? One of the most effective exercises you can do to define your priorities is to write your own eulogy. A eulogy is the speech that someone close to you gives at the celebration of life after you have left this world. What would you want people to say about you? How do you want to be remembered? What is the legacy you want to leave behind after you are gone? Once you write your eulogy, ask yourself this important question: *Are my goals, time, and energy aligned with how I want to be remembered?* I'm guessing your eulogy will not include statements like, "She worked 50+ hours a week and made a lot of money" but rather something like "She was an amazing mother, friend, mentor, and colleague." Take a look at your eulogy and your vision side by side. Is there alignment or disconnection? Or do you simply need to reframe your vision to ensure you are nurturing your legacy and priorities?

Reframing Success

Similar to being clear about your priorities, defining what success means to you is paramount to having a happy and balanced life. We have been socialized to believe that success is defined by how much money we earn, what our title is, and how we choose to earn a living. Respect is given to certain professions over others, and again, these tend to be the high-paying ones. This has been the traditional framework for defining success. However, you know as well as I do that there are many wealthy doctors and lawyers out there that are extremely unhappy. Some will even admit that they never really wanted to pursue their current careers but felt obligated to by their culture or their parents — being successful in a respectful career pays them respect; however, it may not make them happy.

Happiness, true fulfilment, and an increase in consciousness can never be achieved by pursuing someone else's definition of success. However, to avoid this very common pitfall, you will need to establish your own definition of success.

I'm not saying your definition of success cannot include income or financial wellness goals because these things are important. What I am saying is that it is valuable to extend your definition to include the other things that truly matter in life.

If, in the eulogy exercise, you wrote about wanting to be remembered as an amazing parent who made your children feel loved and supported, but your definition of success contains only revenue goals, then there is a disconnect. Your definition of success should include all your priorities and things you value. Some of these may include:

- Maintaining your health so you can be vital and enjoy life
- Surrounding yourself with and investing quality time in your good friends
- Volunteering, being of service, or giving back in some way
- Continually growing as a conscious parent so that you can truly support your children in a meaningful way
- Feeling a deep sense of peace and wholeness
- Enjoying enriching experiences or adventures
- Feeling truly and deeply connected to your partner
- Being financially secure and able to provide for the lifestyle you desire

You might notice the aspirations listed above do not include any specific profession or title, yet working towards any of these goals will consciously create success in your life. If you were to reframe success to be a more complete and full definition, what would it include? One important note — you may have heard the quote "comparison is the thief of joy". Remember that as you define what success means to you.

You are a unique and divinely created being. We each have a unique fingerprint like no one else on the planet, and yet we strive to be the same as everyone else. Don't go down the path of comparison; create a definition of success that is right for you. One that aligns with your heart and soul. Your definition of success should not include what others believe success should look like for you. Sure, take some inspiration from others, but also go within for the guidance that is truly yours. Only you truly know the answers.

What do you need to do to get there?

Once you have defined your vision of success, the next step is to define the gap. Where am I now? What do I need to do to get to where I want to be? I like to do this for different parts of my life. Here are two different practices I use to make sure I am aligned:

1. **New Year's Journal**
   Each year around New Year's, I get out a special journal that I use to make and review each year's goals or intentions. I begin by looking back at what I set out as intentions for the previous year. I then set intentions in the following areas for the year ahead: health, family, work, relationships and love, and travel and adventure.

2. **Success Maps**
   Each year on my birthday, which conveniently falls halfway through the calendar year, I review and revise my Suc-

cess Maps. I have one for each of the following areas in my life: My Financial Success Map, My Health Success Map, My Business Success Map, and my intention statement on the life partner I desire to attract into my life.

Each Success Map includes:

1. Where am I now?

2. Where do I want to be?

3. Why do I want to be there?

4. What do I need to do to get there?

My intention statement on the life partner I want to attract includes a list of desired qualities and the way this person will make me feel. The second piece of this is the answer to, "Who do I need to be in order to attract this type of partner?" In the practice of developing "The List", this second piece is often missing but is still very important as it is actually within my circle of influence.

Room for Magic

I have learned over the years that it is common for us to play small. As we are all on a path to truly discovering our own self-worth and learning how to love ourselves, we sometimes set our vision lower than what is possible or attach ourselves to outcomes that are not truly in our highest and best good. I always recommend when you are setting your intentions that you include a disclaimer such as, "this that I am co-creating **or something better**". Allow space for the universe to help you create something even better than what you can currently imagine.

CHAPTER 9
Creating Space

"When you let go, you create space for something better."
Lori Deschene

Now that you have developed a beautiful vision for what you will achieve and you have worked on your Success Maps to further define your goals, it's time to go deeper. Now we are going to work towards proactively enhancing your power by increasing your levels of consciousness.

The first step in this process is to create space for your vision by letting go of things that no longer serve you and simply take up space in each of the four realms, physical, mental, emotional, and spiritual.

I want you to think about your closet. If I told you that I was giving you five fabulous new outfits, would there be space in your closet? Or is it jam-packed with clothes that are out of style or that you are hoping may fit one day? Think about this for a minute — do those skinny jeans really inspire you and change your behaviours to lose weight? Or do they just make you feel sad that they no longer fit, and you beat yourself up because they don't? This is a perfect example of something in your life that is no longer serving you; you can't wear the jeans, and they lower your vibration because they create negative emotions. So why are you holding onto them? Make room for those five fabulous new outfits!

Letting go is hard. Trust me, it is one of the hardest things I have ever had to learn to do. Apparently, people born under my star sign, Cancer, are the most challenged in the "letting go" department, so I have lots of experience. In my early twenties, my boyfriend wanted to go skydiving for his birthday. As a self-proclaimed scaredy-cat, this was a big deal for me. But my emotional need to connect with my partner, supporting his dreams and desires, created a purpose that drove me past the fear.

So, off we went. It was a Saturday morning, and we went to a field in a small town in Alberta near where I was born and raised. Fortunately, we spent most of the day learning what to do, over and over again; this was partially so we would be safe, but more so to build the champion mindset needed to throw our bodies out of an airplane high in the sky and to trust that the flimsy cloth called a parachute would in fact do its job and get us safely to the ground.

Once we were all prepared for the experience, we loaded into a small six-seater airplane and took off. When we approached the correct altitude, the instructor opened the side door and the wind gushed in, immediately taking my breath away. Two or three people went ahead of me. Then, my turn came. I approached the open door, and, with a lot of encouragement, I grasped onto the wing of the plane and inched myself out to where I was supposed to be. My fingers were tightly clenched to the wing, holding on for dear life. I was so afraid! If I let go, would I indeed survive? Could I just stay there forever clenching onto the wing of that plane? As my mind swirled, the instructor, sensing I was not going to let go on my own, smacked at my fingers, forcing me to release. I felt my stomach drop to the tips of my toes in the free fall. But then, as soon as my chute opened, something incredible happened. The fear turned to awe. I could see for miles as I gently floated in the sky. I felt like I was flying! I felt free, liberated from the torture I had quite literally experienced in anticipating the jump. I landed safely and felt totally and completely invigorated. Will I ever do it again? Hell, no! But from that day forward, this experience represents a perfect example of letting go.

Letting go is one of the most difficult things to do in life.

This is not surprising since we humans spend our lives in search of safety, connection, and comfort. The process of letting go usually means there will be, even if for a short time, a void or empty space in our lives until whatever we have let go of is replaced with something better. The challenge lies in not having a crystal ball to show us what will come to replace that void. Something better always comes, but we are not built or conditioned to trust in the natural flow of the universe.

A theory in human behaviour is that the only thing worse than bad is uncertainty. When we let go, we are choosing to put ourselves into a space of uncertainty. This is why it is so common not to let go. Not letting go feels like the safer option because it is certain. We trust certainty over the possibility of better.

Whether your journey involves letting go of a career path, a passion, a hobby, or a relationship, at some point there was joy, hope, and potential. We believe either the way things are will always remain the same or that things will continue to grow and improve; the last thing we want to believe is that things will evolve, change, or simply fizzle out because of a misalignment.

Letting go is also difficult because it involves intentionally placing ourselves into a grieving process, allowing a former vision that we were attached to die. When what we had previously imagined or believed is no longer feasible, it is natural to feel a sense of loss or grief. So, we avoid the short-term pain of uncomfortable emotions and choose to hold on tight.

Another challenge we face in letting go is our cultural conditioning around never giving up. We are taught that strength comes from perseverance and that there is no space for the natural ebb and flow of life, the evolution and progress of creating something better and more aligned as we naturally grow.

When my daughter was around five years old, we registered her for violin lessons. As a highly committed parent who wanted nothing but the best for my children, I believed that by enrolling her in music lessons, I was making the best decision to support her future. All the good parents were doing this, so clearly if my daughter had a music education, she would have a much more successful future. Additionally, I had heard of the correlation between music and excelling in mathematics, a subject which had always been difficult for me. Violin appeared to be the instrument of choice as Ally loved Yoko, the violin-playing cat from a children's TV show called Timothy Goes to School. *I did some research and located an excellent music school thirty minutes away. Every Saturday morning, we scrambled around to arrive at her lesson on time. Our instructor was wonderful, and we enjoyed our time with him immensely; however, the struggle in between our visits for Ally to practise daily, and the extreme anxiety on recital days (to the point of vomiting on her pretty dress) signalled it was time to let go. It took me about a year to get past the "you can't just give up when things are hard" programming to realize that this was not adding value to anyone's life; despite the possibility of being viewed as a "quitter", it was time to let go. Saying goodbye to our gifted instructor was hard. He was such a wonderful and extremely talented musician, but even more so, a patient and kind person.*

But what happens when you let go? You make room for something better.

Before long, Ally started dance which became her passion. She loved it and not once did she say she did not want to go. She danced four times a week, was a part of the competitive team, and loved her teachers and fellow dancers as well as competing and performing. My baby girl, who was so anxious to the point of vomiting on violin recital day, performed like a bright light at dance competitions and on recital days. There was so much joy which translated to so much growth and positive development in her confidence and self-esteem over time. And despite not being able to play an instrument or sing, Ally has always excelled in mathematics. In Grade 7, she ranked in the top 10% in the province in standardized testing. Today, she is an elementary educator who is highly passionate about and excels at teaching math.

In order for this to happen, I had to let go of a lot — the societal expectation to not give up and the fear of being perceived as a quitter as well as a belief about what being a good parent looked like. Thank heavens I "gave up"! Thank heavens I decided to "quit"! Thank heavens I put us into that space of uncertainty of what would come next. Would she find a talent or hobby she could be passionate about and that would support her growth and development? It would have been easy to say the right thing to do was to be persistent, to keep showing up, developing grit, pushing through ... but that was definitely not the right thing for us, and I knew it in my gut. Letting go of what was not working or serving her was one of the best parenting decisions I have ever made because it created the space for something better.

I have never experienced a situation where when I felt like I had to let go, it led me to a worse outcome. Yet stepping into the uncertain feelings in between letting go and finding what is next feels so difficult. When I trust in the reality that uncertainty is actually a place of possibility and trust that I am aligned and on the path of my divine purpose, it helps me breathe and move forward.

Becoming more comfortable with letting go is a vital step as you elevate to a more conscious state. Being able to identify things, feelings, or behaviours in your life that are causing more stress than joy or simply filling up space and not allowing new fresh things to enter creates a barrier to ease, flow, and joy.

Let's now look at all four realms to identify areas where we may be able to do some "letting go".

Creating Physical Freedom

If letting go in the physical realm is a challenge for you, one clue might be that you have a lot of stuff. Your desk may be overloaded and messy, your closet crowded with clothes you never wear, and your storage space full of things you never use but believe that you may need one day. Or possibly another way you are challenged to let go in the physical realm shows up as a struggle to maintain a healthy body weight.

As we discussed in Chapter 5, the realms play in symphony, that is, they are always influenced by each other. Our attachment to physical things is usually linked to the emotional or spiritual (our unconscious mind) realms and a fear of not being safe. All of us have fears, whether they are conscious or unconscious, that relate to feelings of safety or security. Attachment in the physical realm can indicate fears around safety, security, money, and abundance and when these emotions are left unprocessed or unhealed, extra body weight can result and lead to other physical ailments.

In fact, carrying extra body weight is usually a sure sign that there is more going on than just a basic physical response. Additional body weight is a subconscious layer of protection. Unhealed emotion not only drives unhealthy habits like poor nutrition, overconsumption of food, alcohol, and sugar and a lack of motivation to exercise but also creates a lack of ease which starts to affect our cells and create a state of "dis-ease".

I have struggled at several points in my life to maintain a healthy body weight. The times when the scale was the highest can be directly linked to times of emotional upheaval. The first time I can recall having an issue with my weight was not long after my first wedding when I was in my mid 20s. Up to that point, I had been extremely active, thin, and fit. But once I was married and working in my sedentary office job, my focus shifted from a carefree lifestyle that included fun and a few dance classes a week to adulting. I was a new wife just beginning a career in a very tough job market. I had to work hard to outshine the competition. In addition, my spouse's career was in an initial building stage which took him away from home for up to six months at a time. I remember feeling very alone and unsupported. The combination of less physical movement, the increased pressures of adulthood, and the low-vibration emotion of loneliness caused me to gain weight. Since then, my weight has yo-yoed over the years based on how happy and secure (or alternatively, stressed and insecure) I felt.

My highest weight was when I was in a relationship that was not going anywhere despite how badly I wanted it to. I was doing everything I could to force things, and each day I felt frustrated that I was not seeing the momentum or outcomes I desired. I felt like I had invested so much in the relationship already and was holding on believing happiness would come if I could just be patient. As I held on to the hope things would get better, my body held onto more and more weight. When I realized that this relationship was never going to flourish and decided to let go, my body exhaled, relaxed, and released thirty pounds. It was definitely not easy as I felt this relationship was meant for me. I was holding on so tight that I failed to step back and see that I was not getting my own needs met and that no matter how much I loved this person, love is sometimes not enough.

Let's now look at what you can do to let go in the physical realm that will help not only create space for new and wonderful things but also support your health and well-being.

Letting Go in the Physical Realm

1. Clean your spaces

Your office, closet, refrigerator, and storage space — if you haven't used something in the last year and do not think you will in the next year, do you really need it? To paraphrase Marie Kondo, professional organizer, take each item in hand and ask yourself, "Does this spark joy?" If the answer is yes, keep it. If the answer is no, dispose of it. Donate or sell the stuff you no longer need as it is simply clogging up your energy. I believe in the cycle of abundance and prefer to donate things I no longer need. Although I may not make an immediate return on my investment like I might if I sold the item on Facebook Marketplace, I know that when I give, it opens up space to receive in other completely unrelated ways.

2. Clean your diet

Is there anything you are consuming in your diet that may have a negative effect on you? Different foods and substances affect people in different ways. Being mindful of how certain foods affect you is a good way to identify how you may benefit by removing them from your diet. Dark circles under your eyes the day after eating a specific food may signal an allergy or sensitivity. Another way to identify if certain foods may not be right for you is if they make you feel tired one to three hours after consuming them. Do you get the "booze blues" the day after you drink alcohol? What foods do you crave? Do you know why you are craving these foods? Be your own detective. Continuing to consume foods that we have sensitivities to causes chronic inflammation in our bodies that can lead to disease.

3. Clean your refrigerator

When you are reviewing what you are consuming in your diet, a positive thing to do is clean your refrigerator. Are there leftovers that you are never going to eat? Are there sauces or condiments that expired a long time ago? Let go of these things. Toss out anything that you are never going to use. Then organize your fridge so you can simply open the door and easily find what you need; use the new freed-up space to stock up on highly nutritious foods that will fuel your body.

4. Identify other negative factors

What else in your physical world might you be consuming that has a negative effect on you, lowers your energy, or makes you feel bad? Personally, I stopped watching the news years ago because as a sensitive person, it only fed my fear and anxiety, and much of the information was outside of my circle of influence anyway. Are their friendships or relationships in your personal or professional lives that bring more negative or destabilizing feelings? Consider if letting these go may be in your best interests.

5. Identify your addictions

What are your addictions? Addictions are physical attachments to activities or substances that act as a coping response to numb the conscious or unconscious pain of unhealed emotions. Common addictions include alcohol, sugar, overeating, drugs, pornography, sex, running, or extreme exercising. We become addicted as the substance or action either dulls our ability to feel or floods our physical bodies with feel-good chemicals like dopamine and oxytocin.

Letting go in the physical realm is difficult because our attachments in this realm are complex and include unresolved emotion from other realms. However, that being said, it's a good place to begin to create awareness. Our body is the home for our brain, heart, and soul, and it responds to the health and well-being of these. When we can listen to our bodies and understand what they are responding to, we can use that knowledge to get to the root of our challenges and start creating balance.

Creating Mental Freedom

One of the most common challenges leaders are faced with is the feeling of overwhelm. There are so many things to do and so many things to remember! Although overwhelm happens in the mental realm, it inevitably leads to physical realm challenges like anxiety and struggling to get a deep, restful sleep. The mind-body connection doesn't take long to kick in. Being stuck in our minds can be a very painful place to be.

I remember the chaos I experienced in the mental realm when I was deciding if I should leave my first marriage. I was in a place of deep sadness and did not feel supported, loved, or even seen. My husband was my junior high school sweetheart and because we had known each other for so long, I definitely had feelings of being taken for granted. Once, after returning from working out of town for a long period, he opted to go on vacation with his parents while I stayed home and worked — the writing was on the wall! Or perhaps it was when he suggested we label the food we each buy in the refrigerator so that his contribution to the grocery bill would be protected while he was away. When I suggested counselling, he suggested I go on my own, so I did. I remember in the first session saying, "I do not know if I am here to fix my marriage or end it." Thoughts of, "This is a failure", "I do not want to be a 'divorcée'", "What about all our friends?", "But I love his family" swirled. It felt as though I was standing on the edge of a high diving board, looking down at the water and scared to death to jump. But when I did jump, I felt the biggest sense of relief. I was finally out of the chaos of my mind and moving forward in action towards what was best for me and likely both of us in that moment of decision.

Another common unconscious mental realm challenge that often presents is our need to be right. We live in a highly divided society where we place labels on everything so that we know our position and where we feel safe. The structures in place to guide us like government, education, and (heavens forbid!) the media fuel us to stand strong and fight for what we believe is right. These labels can divide us as we assume a level of superiority or righteousness based on these thoughts. We think that letting go of these thoughts will cause us harm or put us in unsafe territory, so we cling to and affirm what we believe is right.

Imagine if we let go of being right or of what we think is right. Imagine if being a woman, a Black person, a gay person, or a person of a certain religious affiliation was viewed simply as **human** rather than different in a negative or threatening way. What if these humans did not have to "fight" to be seen as equal or valuable? This is the divine truth, and yet, our need to think, classify, and divide to protect our own thoughts so that we can be right is driven by fear and lower-level unconscious behaviours.

Being open-minded by responding to others with, "That's interesting. I've never thought about it that way. Tell me more," is a hard thing to do. Most of the time, we respond by asserting our own position to convince someone they are off track and that **we** are in fact right. Humans have a deep desire to be right; expanding our understanding or feeling safe amid a multitude of opinions is rare. The lack of a strong position is somehow incorrectly linked to a lack of confidence. As you grow in consciousness, you are more apt to consider that there is more than just black or white and right or wrong; you start to look for understanding as opposed to taking a divided approach.

You begin to let go of the need to be right and start thinking from a more conscious space.

Let's now look at some things you can do to let go in the mental realm that will help you not only create space for new and wonderful things but will also support your health and well-being.

Letting Go in the Mental Realm

1. Have a list

Write everything you need to do on a list, in a notebook, or on a piece of paper. Then start actioning them one by one. Once you complete a task, check it off and feel the sense of accomplishment that will provide momentum to move on to the next task with positive energy. Overwhelm is often caused by our mind being overloaded with all the things we need to remember to do. We lose sleep because we are afraid we will forget to do something. Just like hoarders who keep too much stuff in their house, many people fill their minds with their to-do lists. By getting these thoughts out of your head and onto paper, you can free up headspace to think clearly and feel more in control of everything you have on the go.

2. Use the Circle of Influence

In his book *The 7 Habits of Highly Effective People*, Stephen Covey speaks to the theory of the Circle of Influence, a very powerful model when applied. The basic idea is that we all have a Circle of Concern that includes all of the things in life we are concerned about. When we focus and spend time thinking about the things in our Circle of Concern, it can become overwhelming and, in turn, ineffective. However, within that Circle of Concern, we also have a Circle of

Influence that includes things that are within our control or actions we can take towards things that are concerning us. When we focus on our Circle of Influence, it naturally expands, and we begin to feel much more empowered. For example, global warming may be in your Circle of Concern. It's a real threat that can impact our lives as well as those of future generations on Planet Earth for centuries to come. If this is something you are concerned about and it takes up mind space thinking about it, consider what is in your Circle of Influence. What action can you take to let this go from your mind? Can you join a group? Can you vote for parties who have a plan and are committed to making progress? Can you make a financial donation to a cause that is making advances? Can you intentionally meditate alone or in a group with the intention of healing Mother Gaia? There are many different options that may work well for you if you focus on what is in your Circle of Influence rather than letting your concern about this issue place you in a disempowered state of fear and overwhelm.

3. **Make decisions and take action**

It is very easy to get stuck in analysis paralysis or over-thinking the obstacles and challenges we all naturally face. This can not only be confusing but also exhausting; it typically leads to a downward spiral of more analysis and more confusion. I call this being stuck in the dance, a space of indecision. Can you think of a time when you were stuck in a place of indecision but then were finally able to decide? How did that make you feel? Once we arrive at a decision, it creates a feeling of freedom. Freedom from the torturous hamster wheel in our mind. Just like when I finally decided to leave my first marriage. Once the decision was made, months of resistance and pain evaporated. Analysis paralysis can last months, years, or even lifetimes.

When you are having trouble making a decision, it is best to set a deadline. You may need to extend your deadline, but without one, you may stay stuck in indecision forever. Then, use the time to weigh pros and cons, determine impacts, and assess potential actions and their ability to meet your needs. If there are consequences, how can you mitigate these? Failing to make decisions will lead you to a state of resistance or lack of ease that will ultimately create "dis-ease" in your body. Being decisive, taking action, and moving forward are all important acts of self-care.

4. Shift realms

When you are stuck in a negative cycle of overanalysing, and you are unable to make a decision, it is very effective to step out of the mind and sink into the heart for guidance. Simply close your eyes, place your hand on your heart, take a few deep breaths and think, *What is in the highest and best good for everyone involved?* Allow the answers to present themselves. You may not get an answer immediately; however, remain open for clarity to present itself in the coming hours or days. If you are open, the answers will become clear.

Letting go in the mental realm can be a game-changer; when we fail to do so, we become more anxious and exhausted, creating a pattern that can catch on like wildfire and prevent you from clearly and wisely moving forward to achieve the success you deserve.

Creating Emotional Freedom

The emotional realm is where we struggle the most to let go. We are often never taught how to honour our emotions, so we suck it up, soldier on, and push our unprocessed emotions aside. In survival mode, we will do just about anything to move forward and avoid pain or uncomfortable feelings that we simply do not know how to process. These stored emotions are where our triggers and insecurities manifest. We believe that because we have avoided our emotions, they have no impact on us; however, the exact opposite is true. These triggers and insecurities greatly impact the way we show up in the world. How we are perceived by others in our professional and personal lives ultimately affects our ability to achieve our desires.

Letting Go in the Emotional Realm

1. Identify and process emotion

I am fairly certain that each of us was either punished for a display of emotion or rewarded for **not** displaying uncomfortable emotions in order to act appropriately at some point in our childhood. Although we cannot go through life outwardly displaying our emotions all the time, we also need to understand that avoiding emotions will not release them. Failure to process and release our emotional responses typically results in negative outcomes from triggered outbursts, physical disease, or simply not showing up in a positive, balanced way that will ultimately affect our success.

You know when you are feeling off, anxious, or sad. Or you may be soldiering on under a whitewash of positivity until someone cuts you off in traffic; then all the emotion you have managed to stuff down in recent months comes bursting to the surface in anger. Where does that unreasonably high level of anger come from? It's simple — it's all of the emotions that have previously been ignored.

Integrating a practice where you can check in with your-self and identify both what you are feeling and the root of that feeling will help you process it so it can be released and leave your energy field. Many people have great success working with a therapist or counsellor as they act as a guide to draw out the emotion, talk things through, and help you process negative emotions.

2. Forgiveness practice

Life happens. People hurt us, maybe intentionally or maybe not. However, it is through the lens with which we choose to view the hurt and our ability to heal the pain that we can be greatly impacted. The natural human response is to hold on to the hurts to protect us from experiencing that pain again. The problem is that when we remain in a guarded state, we not only prevent our body from being at ease, which again can create physical "dis-ease", but we are also prevented from being in an open state to receive abundance. As Marianne Williamson says, "Not forgiving is like drinking poison and waiting for the other person to die."

Although we may think that not forgiving will hold the other person accountable for their transgressions, the truth is we only harm ourselves. I have also heard people say, "I will forgive, but not forget." Although it is good to take our lessons, use them in context, and apply them to our future choices and decisions, not forgetting holds onto this negative and restrictive energy in our energy field and manifests as resentment. My best advice is to shift from "I will forgive, but not forget," to "I receive the lessons with gratitude and bless and release the negative and restrictive emotions related to this situation."

My favourite forgiveness practice is to write a letter to the person you are struggling to forgive. Write them a letter and let all of your thoughts and emotions flow through you onto the paper. It might take many pages. Keep going and say everything you need to say until there is nothing left. If tears emerge during the process, don't hold back — let them all out. Then, take your piece of paper, fold it in half and then in half again. Go to a place where you can safely light your paper on fire and watch it burn. As the paper burns, feel the release while the emotions and energy transmute and try to imagine something you are grateful for that this person taught you. Give thanks for the lessons, and ... let it go.

Next, think about writing a letter to yourself. What do you need to forgive yourself for? Bad decisions, bad choices, not being in your power, letting others' opinions and emotions matter more than yours, not taking care of or honouring yourself? Whatever you may feel (anger or disappointment in yourself), forgive and release. Often these are the most impactful feelings and, once released, can make you feel significantly lighter.

3. Letting go of fear and anxiety

Fear is likely my most constant companion; I have spent the greater part of my life in conversation and negotiation with it. I am quite confident that prior to any of my life's achievements, I had to work through a lot of fear and doubt. I have come to realize this will likely always be the case, so rather than try to fight the fear, I just need to invite it along for the ride. I move forward in spite of the fear rather than resisting it. The winning formula is to allow fear to be present while I continue to make progress rather than allowing it to shut me down.

There are a few things that I use to let go of my fear and anxiety. The first is to focus on my purpose. When you have a clear purpose and understand why you want to do or achieve something, the light of purpose becomes more powerful than the darkness of fear. The fear doesn't go away, but the purpose motivates and helps move you forward. When you feel inspired to do something but fear arises, take some time and ask yourself, *What is the purpose of this desire? Why do I want to achieve this? What will the outcome be if I am successful? What will the outcome be if I am not?* If the purpose is strong, your confidence and courage will increase, and you will naturally release some of the fear to make space for inspiration and action.

Another effective way to release fear and anxiety is through movement. You can either move your body or take action on specific items on your to-do list. The idea is to move the stagnant, negative energy that may be keeping you stuck in a spiral of limiting emotion. This is another example of the connection between the realms, linking the physical (move your body) or mental (take action on your list of things to do) to release emotions (such as fear and anxiety). When you move your body, there is an increase in your brain's powerful feel-good neurotransmitters called endorphins. If hitting the gym is your vibe, go for it! But if not, then head out for a walk, do some stretching, or turn on some upbeat music that lifts your spirits and dance in your living room. Feel your destabilizing, low-vibration emotions move through and out of you.

Another highly effective way to address fear and anxiety is through balancing your root chakra. We will learn more about the chakras, what they are, and how powerful they can be when balanced in Chapter 11 — Becoming a Servant Leader.

A Note About Grief

Grief is likely the most difficult emotion for any of us to process. They say that the amount of grief you experience is proportionate to how much you loved someone. But we also experience grief when we are attached to ideas or outcomes that do not play out like we had hoped. Understand that when you are grieving the loss of a person or of an idea or vision you had hoped would come to fruition, letting go is not easy. In fact, it can be a lifelong process, and that's okay. I liken processing grief to peeling an onion. It comes in layers. When you are healing from such a loss, give yourself lots of time, patience, support, and grace.

A Note About Anger

Anger is a secondary emotion, meaning that when you feel anger, there is a primary emotion that is actually fuelling it. In order to let go of your anger, you will need to get to the root of it by asking yourself, *What emotion am I feeling beneath my anger? Am I frustrated, scarred, humiliated, hurt or rejected?* Find the root cause and then work through the release of that emotion.

Creating Spiritual Freedom

My spiritual journey has been interesting to say the least. Up until my sister died, I went to the United Church with my family regularly and attended Sunday School. However, after she passed away, my parents were angry with God. They could not understand or process how an all-loving God could ever put them through a child's death. Fair. To call it unfair would be an understatement. As a result, at age four, my religious path ceased.

In university, I pledged Alpha Omicron Pi, a women's fraternity, and felt deeply connected to and uplifted by the Ritual — a secret spiritual practice that bonded us sisters together and to our inspired values in a deep and meaningful way. I loved the way the Ritual made me feel. How it transcended my thoughts and feelings which in my early twenties were still quite tumultuous and, frankly, all over the map. The Ritual grounded me. Centred me. Empowered me. It was precisely what my soul had been craving for a long time.

Throughout the years, I have realized that I have been receiving signs from Spirit. Whenever I felt sad or when something important happened, I would see a rabbit. When I visited my sister's grave, there were rabbits. The day I found out I was being promoted from management trainee to my first Human Resources role, I was in the office and received a call from the general manager, Scott, offering me the promotion. Right after the call, I left the office to get lunch and right there in the parking lot bluff was a rabbit. It wasn't long after my daughter was born when we realized her Chinese zodiac sign is the Rabbit. As they say, "Coincidences are God's way of remaining anonymous." For many years now, I have been open to receiving signs from beyond the 3-D earth plane and fully trust that there is something more out there supporting us.

After university and a few years into my career, I took a promotion and moved to the west coast of Canada. My soul craved being close to the ocean, the softer, more rounded mountains, the diversity of beautiful colours, and the vital life and expansiveness

*I feel each time I breathe in the west coast air. After my reloca-
tion, I was on my own and knew virtually no one, except for
one sorority sister, Marjorie, whom I had met at a few inter-
national conventions and who was kind enough to nurture my
transition to a new city. Although I was delighted with my new
career opportunity and to be living in one of the best places in
Canada, a part of me felt very alone. I was drawn to a beautiful
United Church in my neighbourhood; attending services there
provided that feeling of being grounded, centred, and at peace
within my soul.*

*Not long after I was married, in that same church, we moved
to the suburbs to start a family. We tried attending a United
church in our new neighbourhood, but it did not resonate, so
we began attending an Anglican church in the same area; once
again, I found that sense of connection, both to the commun-
ity and to my spiritual practice. But it wasn't long before my
marriage began to falter, and my husband found the time com-
mitment of the Anglican practice too long and in conflict with
his passion for the National Football League.*

*In a serious attempt to improve my marriage and to have my
family spiritually aligned, I began an intensive 8-month pro-
cess to convert to Catholicism. When we were initially married,
I was adamant that I would never convert as there were certain
Catholic church beliefs that were not aligned with my own val-
ues or belief systems. However, at this point in my marriage, I
thought being on the same religious team was important, so I
compromised. I focused on some very exceptional and wonder-
ful people in my life who were Catholic and was led by their
example, as opposed to thinking about my own misalignment.
I set myself aside for what I felt was a greater good.*

The converting process was very challenging. Imagine being thirty-two years old and undergoing the ritual of First Confession. A practice that felt completely out of alignment to begin with went horribly wrong. My First Confession was scheduled on the same afternoon I had to conduct a mass reduction in workforce at my job. Following this emotionally exhausting event, I drove to the church to jump through the next hoop in my journey to become a Catholic. The priest told me to meet him at the house. I assumed that we would walk over to the church together and that I would kneel on the other side of the little wall in the confessional booth; this would protect me somewhat as I revealed over three decades worth of shameful acts. However, when I got to his house, Father invited me into the living room, and I sat on a chair across the room in plain sight — no wall, no kneeling, no ability to shift my gaze of shame downward. There I was in the plain light of day ready to confess all my sins. The highlight was when I confessed that I had engaged in pre-marital sex, and Father responded by asking me how many times. I lied. I lied in my First Confession because the experience did not feel safe or right. My god, Source, the universe already knows everything I have done, the good, the bad, and the ugly and still loves and accepts me.

I completed all of the steps, became a Catholic, and practised for several years. My favourite part was the deep and structured rituals of Mass that always helped me to feel connected and in alignment to God/Source. My children went to a wonderful Catholic elementary school where they received an excellent education. I am extremely grateful for the opportunity this provided them to develop their own sense of faith and an understanding of something powerful, supportive, and magical outside of themselves. I am also grateful for the contributions to my own spiritual journey. In the end, it did not save my marriage, and, as a divorced person, I no longer felt welcome in the Catholic church. I felt judged, not by God, but by the religion. Hence, I am no longer a practicing Catholic.

My path has been an interesting one. What I have learned through the steps and stages of my spiritual journey is that I need to feel that connection to something outside of myself; however, I do not require another person or religious organization to facilitate that for me. I have everything I require within me to have a deeply connected relationship with Spirit. My current spiritual practice feels deeper than anything I have experienced to date. I practise meditation daily and feel my connection to Source at all times, not just during my meditation practice. I am aware of the signs and synchronicities and believe I am co-creating my best life with the support of a powerful and all-knowing force.

Understand that we all have our own unique spiritual journey and that many people have positive experiences through their religious practice. In no way do I mean to use my own experience to diminish that. It is important to do what works best for you. Historically, people's spiritual beliefs have divided humanity, and the need to be right and powerful has caused many conflicts and much bloodshed. It is my belief that it is in the spiritual realm where the differentiation or extra edge lies, and as a result, unconscious human fear of this realm drives a need to either abolish or control it. Countless religious wars are waged in the quest to be right. There is a lack of openness and tolerance for other ways to believe or practise our connection to the spiritual realm because we naturally respond with fear to things that are different from what we know.

Letting go in the spiritual realm can be difficult for many because the concept of what constitutes "spiritual" is confusing. Let me try my best to simplify it for you.

The spiritual realm is the space beyond us, that which we cannot see or touch, but that we can most certainly interact with. It's a belief in something powerful and supportive outside ourselves. You might practise your spirituality through a lens of religion, or you might be like me and practise your spirituality independently and without an intermediary. Or you might consider yourself an atheist and have a vision which you are not yet able to see or touch but is still housed in your spiritual realm.

The spiritual realm includes our beliefs, what we believe to be true both consciously and unconsciously. Letting go of beliefs that no longer serve you can transform the way the world responds to you and help you to develop more freedom, peace, and ease.

Letting Go in the Spiritual Realm

1. Shadow Work

Shadow work allows you to call forward things from your unconscious mind into your conscious awareness and to process thoughts and emotions that have previously stagnated and held you back. You can work with a practitioner who will lead you through the shadow work prompts; however, I think the self-directed journalling approach is also highly effective. All you have to do is begin with a journal and the shadow work questions as your guide. You can simply Google many different options for questions. Don't overthink this exercise; choose a source you feel drawn to rather than reading every option and analysing what is the best. You may want to start with a fresh journal specifically for your shadow work and commit to doing a certain number of prompts in a certain time frame, for example, one a day or three a week. You should set aside time when you will not be interrupted and create a sacred space by lighting a candle, bringing a blanket and a warm cup of tea, or whatever makes you feel safe and supported.

Here are some examples of shadow work prompts:

- Which parts of myself do I judge?
- What do I dislike about others?
- What do I admire most about others?
- When do I feel triggered?
- Where is this trigger coming from?
- When in the past have I felt similarly? (In time, you'll begin to see patterns in your thinking and behaviour that lead to the core wound.)
- What are the emotions I find difficult to let myself feel?
- Where in my body do I feel these emotions?
- What do I do to cope with difficult emotions?
- Are these coping mechanisms benefiting me?
- What feeling do I want to achieve through this coping mechanism?
- Which emotions were invalidated during my childhood?
- Do I reject any traits that I see in my parents?
- What would I change about my parents?

2. Automatic Writing

As in shadow work journalling, where you write in response to prompts, automatic writing is a process in which you have a question on your mind that you are seeking clarity about, and you allow whatever comes through you to emerge on the paper. All you need is a piece of paper, a pen, and a quiet space. Then, intentionally ask a question and begin writing. Allow yourself to write until you feel done. You may come back a few days later and ask if there is anything else and write some more. It is good to wait for a few days and then go back and read what came through you. I find this is a great process to bypass the mind when you feel stuck in overanalysing or thinking obsessively.

3. Spiritual Practices or Therapies

There are many different options to heal and let go of negative or limiting beliefs. I have experienced many and prefer the following approaches as they clear and release elements that may not be in my conscious mind. Often, they can be released without needing to fully draw out, talk through, or understand them. To me, these types of healing modalities are like a Fast Pass at Disneyland; rather than getting on a ride faster, you are letting go and healing whatever is holding you back from being your best and most healthy self.

These modalities include Reiki, Subconscious Release Technique, Theta Healing, Emotion Code, childhood and past life regression, and meditation. Most of these practices work on your whole being — your physical, mental, emotional, and spiritual bodies and also include ancestral clearing. Read on for a brief description of each of these alternative therapies.

Reiki

Reiki is a Japanese technique for stress reduction and relaxation that also promotes healing. It is administered by "laying on hands" and is based on the idea that an unseen "life force energy" flows through us and is what causes us to be alive. If one's "life force energy" is low, then we are more likely to get sick or feel stress, and if it is high, we are more capable of being happy and healthy. The word "reiki" is made up of two Japanese words, "rei" which means "wisdom or the Higher Power" and "ki" which is "life force energy," so reiki actually means "spiritually guided life force energy".

[Source - Reiki.org]

Subconscious Release Technique (SRT)

SRT is a powerful brain-coding technique rooted in behavioural science that allows people to completely reprogram negative thought patterns and bias and neutralize emotional blocks. It is based on research that dates from the 1970s by Lester Levenson, a physicist who discovered this profound approach to overcoming our deep-seated, limiting beliefs. The goal of SRT is to create a mindset that focuses on opportunity, purpose, and healthful relationships and to promote more consistent feelings of positivity, possibility, and joy. By engaging in this technique, we are able to construct mental pathways that empower us to begin accessing our greater potential and create the life we truly want to be living.

[Source - loveignitespeace.com]

Theta Healing

Theta Healing is a meditation technique and spiritual philosophy that uses focused thought and prayer. This technique offers physical, emotional, and spiritual healing by tapping into the Theta brain wave and connecting with Source. When we experience this connection, we can reprogram our minds to clear limiting beliefs and think positively. This brings out the best in ourselves and allows us to live our most enlightened, successful lives.

[Source - thetahealing.com]

Emotion Code

The Emotion Code is a simple and fast method to find and remove negative emotional energy from the body. It uses kinesiology or muscle testing to connect to the subconscious mind and to find out where the blockages are and what emotions they are related to. Then, a magnet is rolled over the corresponding body meridians several times to release those emotional energy blockages. The energies of intense emotional events experienced are still stuck in one's physical body and can distort the normal energy flow, resulting in pain, disease, PTSD, depression, anxiety, phobias, and mental illnesses. The Emotion Code helps release these blockages.

[Source - alternativesforhealing.com]

Regression Therapy

Regression Therapy is an intervention that focuses on uncovering subconscious memories or traumas from your past. It aims to find out the root cause of your present-day thoughts and reactions. Therapists who use this practice may employ techniques like hypnosis to unlock subconscious memories that are directing your current behaviour.

[Source - Psychcentral.com]

Meditation

Meditation is the practice of concentrated focus upon a sound, object, visualization, the breath, movement, or attention itself in order to increase awareness of the present moment, reduce stress, promote relaxation, and enhance personal and spiritual growth. Meditation benefits people with or without medical illness or stress. People who meditate regularly have been shown to feel less anxiety and depression. They also report that they experience more enjoyment and appreciation of life and that their relationships with others are improved. Meditation produces a state of deep relaxation and a sense of balance or equanimity.

[Source - Medicaldictionary.com]

If you are curious about trying any of these practices, I recommend asking a friend for a referral or simply using Google to locate a practitioner in your area. Or you can practise your ability to co-create with Spirit by asking, "Bring me a spiritual practitioner who will help me let go of whatever is holding me back." Then follow the signs — perhaps you will meet someone, a friend will tell you about someone, or you will have an ad pop up in your social media. Follow the signs, and let the magic unfold.

Seasons and Cycles

We have been programmed to always move forward, get results, make things happen, and push for results. Productivity is indeed a very important thing; however, when we understand the rhythms and cycles of life, we can more effectively work with them to find a much more effective and sustainable rhythm.

Just like the seasons, we need periods of pause and of letting go so that we can move forward, plant new seeds, and watch ourselves flourish. Rather than thinking about letting go as a negative, painful experience, I like to take a cue from the season of autumn, when the trees gently and naturally let go of their leaves, trusting fully that although they will stand bare and exposed throughout the winter, in the spring, they will bud and blossom even larger than they did the year before.

Another example of the natural rhythms of life is the cycles of the moon. The moon does not stay in its full moon state, shining bright and lighting up the sky 365 days a year. It naturally and effortlessly moves through cycles each month beginning with the new moon; it lets go of its need to show up and be seen, so that it can begin a new cycle within that darkness. The darkness of the new moon creates a space for something fresh to begin once again to grow to its full and magnificent state.

You are no different, beautiful soul. Allow the cycles. Allow the rhythms of life and let go with ease and grace because you can fully trust that you are completely aligned with the creation of a successful and joy-filled life.

Trust, let go, allow, and you will receive.

CHAPTER 10
Create a New Identity

"Life is not about finding yourself. Life is about creating yourself."
George Bernard Shaw

What if I told you that you have the ability and capacity to create a new identity? Of course, you will still be you, the same perfect, beautiful soul; however, this more conscious version of you will be more empowered and balanced allowing you and everyone around you to confidently shine bright.

Now that you have a good understanding of letting go and have created a space for something new, it's time to create new ways of being so that you can attract the things you really desire. You see, through our experiences we create stories, and as you learned in Chapter 6 - You Are Energy, these stories affect our vibration in either positive or negative ways. By shifting our narratives that keep us stuck in a place of victimization, we can increase our vibration and therefore our experience.

Let me share an example of one of the stories I clung to for a very long time and then show you how rewriting this story enabled me to create a new, more empowered identity.

My Unconscious Story

When my sister died, I felt all alone. I had lost my best friend and soulmate. I had been abandoned. Because my parents were also grieving and trying to survive the worst tragedy anyone could ever imagine, that of losing a child, they were not able to provide the emotional support I needed in those critical moments of my own grief. I had been left "abandoned" by everyone in my tribe — the ones I loved and those who loved me the most. I felt my parents' pain, and the fact that I craved their support only induced feelings of guilt. Being supported and nurtured through this significant time of loss felt needy. So, I withdrew and suffered in silence; I refused to create more pain or draw on my parents' limited reserves. I needed to be strong and put my own feelings and needs aside to keep them safe. If I were to assert my own needs, it might have been too much for them. They may have broken even more. To a point of no return.

Throughout my life, this story has negatively served me in a few different ways. First, there was a belief that if I truly loved someone, they would abandon me. When we have a story, we do everything in our power to prove and validate it. As I mentioned previously, three of my best friends moved away, leaving me to feel abandoned. Clearly these moves were not about me but about excellent opportunities for my friends; however, as I had not altered my story, I allowed them to trigger me and affirm my story.

The second way this story has negatively impacted me is in my pattern to suffer in silence and view my emotional pain or need for support as a burden to others. For a long time, when I was suffering, I simply went missing. I withdrew and worked through things on my own. I did not reach out to friends or talk about my feelings until I had dealt with them.

In relationships, both professional and personal, I tend to be the pleaser, the nurturer, the girl who has her shit together. In romantic relationships, I believed that being a partner who did not require any emotional or financial support made me highly valuable because I was not "needy". My belief was that being needy equals being unworthy and unlovable. I tried to show up as a champion with no needs but a strong ability to provide and give; this placed my relationships in unstable and unbalanced states which ultimately led to them ending. My belief that my emotional needs were a burden led to a fear of receiving. My inability to receive created a block in the natural cycle of abundance of giving and receiving and prevented my relationships from flourishing.

In one of my relationships where I did find the courage to receive, there was a constant fear of the rug being pulled out from under me. At the time, my subconscious fears of not being worthy of the "princess treatment" gave me a constant fear that everything was too good to be true. Rather than enjoy and appreciate the beautiful connection and emotional support that was being offered, fear made me contract which resulted in trying to control outcomes. The attempt to control and hold on for dear life led to the demise of the relationship. I was not ready. Although I had everything I had ever desired, I was not personally healed enough to hold onto this expanded experience.

Shifting to a Conscious Story

In order to create a new identity, to assist with my more abundant and successful future, I needed to shift the stories and beliefs that were holding me back from what my soul was truly craving.

My new story goes like this:

I was sent here with an important purpose in this lifetime. To be a support to and help people overcome their deep pain, grief, and the wounds that limit them from achieving their true potential. To help them shine their brightest. My purpose could not be fulfilled without truly knowing, understanding, and experiencing my own deep pain and the peripheral damage that pain caused. My understanding of how I personally navigated my own healing process now provides a safe and empathetic space for others.

*Yes, it's true. My sister died, and it was extremely sad, unexplainable, and tragic. But I also know without a doubt that ever since she left this earthly plane, she has been by my side helping me grow into my purpose. If I was not alive at the time of her passing, my parents may not have had a much-needed focus, me, their other four-year-old child, to pull them upward and out of the depths of their grief. Both my parents have brought so much light to many people's lives throughout the years. I added value just by being there. I was **supposed** to be there. I was **supposed** to walk a path of deep pain and grief so that when others were feeling the same way, I could be there to support them until they started to see brighter days again. I was **supposed** to struggle in romantic relationships despite having a deep desire to be in a loving, connected, and emotionally supportive partnership so that I would be motivated to continue my healing journey. I was **supposed** to unfold and grow and elevate in consciousness to understand what truly holds people back from the success and abundance they crave so badly. I was **supposed** to be of service so that I can teach what I have learned and help others to thrive.*

Once we understand how our stories develop a narrative that either supports us in achieving our dreams or holds us back in a negative loop that perpetuates the victim mentality ("life is happening to me"), only then can we do a review of the stories we are holding on to and the results they are producing. When we find stories that are not serving our best and highest good, we can then reframe these stories into a more empowered, champion position ("life is happening for me") that will serve us much better.

Depending on your experiences, this can indeed be challenging. However, I promise it is well worth the effort. You already know that the challenging things we do in life often produce the most significant results. After all, the only alternative is to stay stuck in your story and, although that may feel safe and you might even get some sympathy and support, the good feelings achieved from staying stuck are fleeting.

We all know what it's like to scroll through Facebook and see a friend's post sharing their sad news, a meme about how hard life is, or the passive-aggressive posts that anonymously call out the people who they perceive have done them wrong. Our natural instinct as kind and loving humans is to rush in to help. We provide uplifting comments and caring emojis, and the person gets precisely what they feel they need in that moment — love and support. However, we are enabling them to stay stuck in a place of victimhood and to perpetuate an unhealthy pattern of seeking surface level (social media) support, rather than the real, meaningful, and sustainable support that will actually serve them.

What happened to you is not your fault, but it is your responsibility to heal it. Everybody has painful experiences. Everybody has trauma. Our job is to realize that we have the power to step up and transform our challenges and our pain into meaning. Once we let go of the safe yet destructive place of being a vic**tim** of life's circumstances, we transform into the conscious state of becoming a vic**tor** — a champion! It's in this new identity and high-vibrational state where we are able to receive everything we have always wanted.

This is the zone where success starts to find you.

Authentic Leadership

As you begin to rewrite your stories to create your new conscious identity, you will discover a desire to show up as your most authentic self. This is a key ingredient in becoming a conscious leader.

The definition of leadership, in my opinion, is really simple. You are a leader if other people will follow you or if you have the ability to influence others to act or behave in a way you desire. It has nothing to do with your title or how many people report to you. It's simply about your ability to create desirable outcomes through your ability to influence.

In order to influence people, you need to have their trust.

Trust is established through your level of competence and your ability to connect with and support the people you are attempting to influence. When I think of the Unconscious Leader, they assume they are trusted because they have the years of experience or educational qualifications to support their title. However, they are missing the connection and two-way respect the Conscious Leader brings to the table that ultimately builds trust.

For me personally, stepping more into my authentic self has been a long and scary process. For most of my career, I hid half of myself and showed up in a way that I believed would garner respect and help me climb the career ladder. It seemed to work. By being a "get shit done", results-oriented driver that knew what needed to happen, I was able to achieve outcomes. The only challenge was that I often felt exhausted and out of balance. Meanwhile, the other half of me remained tucked away in the closet for fear of judgement or not being respected and, as a result, I was not able to create the life I wanted for my family. I hid away the parts of me that are vulnerable, deeply empathetic, intuitive, highly spiritual, and magical. Most of my clients now know all of me, even the astrology-loving, angel card-reading parts of me! Despite whether they are fully on board with the things I believe in, they trust me because I am fully authentic and wear no masks. They know that despite our difference in beliefs, they can count on me to be real and support them in getting the job done.

I remember being concerned about sharing my authentic self when I was first developing my website. As my company name could already be perceived as "soft", I remember being very particular about the colours. They had to be strong, confident, and corporate. My company name, Glow, represents our truest and brightest potential that can only shine through if we have broken through our challenges and wounds. It's through elevating above these challenges and wounds that we increase our consciousness and become beautiful, glowing beings that are able to reach our highest potential.

Although my purpose was fully aligned to my heart and soul, I was afraid to show up like this. To tone down this spiritual essence, I brought in colours that would show to the world I was serious and results oriented. Version one of my website was red and gold. Strong and powerful. Very yang, male-inspired energy. As I have continued my own growth and conscious elevation and released my fear of being truly authentic, my website has also evolved and now captures my true essence; it incorporates a balance of my yang energy (being strategic, focused, sharp, highly professional, and results oriented) and an allusion to my true super powers and yin energy of being deeply intuitive, conscious, supportive, and empathetic.

Is there a part of you that you are hiding for fear of judgement? Are there masks you wear to protect yourself? Might these masks create walls or decrease your ability to build connections through meaningful trust? Authenticity is even more important as we connect with and lead the next generations. Being real is not just a nice thing to have — it is a critical and foundational expectation for them.

All of You

We have learned that you are not a one-dimensional being. In order to create balance, you need to focus on all of you — your physical, mental, emotional, and spiritual realms. There is another way to look at the diversity that exists in each of us, and that is through the makeup of our divine energy. Each of us has both feminine (yin) and masculine (yang) energies, and in order to capture that elusive balance, we must allow space for both. What typically happens is we tend to lean into one of these energies more than the other — more yin or more yang — which creates a lack of balance and affects the way we are perceived by others.

For most of my corporate career, I worked in male-dominated industries. I looked to the leaders in my work world to define success and I emulated their behaviours and attitudes. This ultimately allowed me to climb the corporate ladder and earn a seat at the table with those male leaders. Looking back, in several of my jobs, I was the only female, but at the time I did not notice this. I was too busy valuing myself as "one of the boys". I had no awareness of the fact that I was shrinking a significant part of myself, the beautiful and powerful divine feminine part of me. I was showing up with a strong yang or divine masculine energy.

As mentioned previously, in 2012, the year before I became an entrepreneur, I had an extremely tough year. My father's passing was significant as he is the person I most closely identify with to this day. He was a deeply feeling person who loved fiercely. He protected and provided. He was a strategic entrepreneur. His legacy continues through me as I work to help others intentionally live up to their highest potential. When I returned home and began working on the mass lay-offs, I flipped a switch. I showed up like a champion, planning and executing a cost-effective strategy and logistics. Everything went smoothly. We made every effort to ensure that everyone impacted was treated with the highest level of respect and dignity. I marched forward and never considered the personal emotional impact of assisting in putting thousands of people out of work.

After completing this work, I was told that I had to significantly downsize my own HR team by more than half. Fortunately, my position was one of a thousand management-level positions across Canada that was selected for elimination. I was offered a promotion and a move, but it would have been back to the

Prairies where I grew up; in addition to being in conflict with my custody agreement, I had absolutely no desire to return there. I had been set free!

I went through an initial unravelling period for several months as I had been accustomed to working so hard for the last five years. I realized I had a low-grade, constant pain on my left side across my ribs. Interestingly, the left side of our body houses our feminine or yin side. It is also where our heart resides. In order to do the work I had to do for the final two years while simultaneously grieving the loss of my father, my body responded by trying to take care of my heart. In order to show up, strategize, and execute, I needed to maximize my masculine, yang energy. Did I do an amazing job? Yes, absolutely, without a doubt. Was I out of balance, frustrated, snippy, and having a physical response in my body as a result? One hundred percent.

Starting my own company did not allow me to show up as my authentic and balanced self on Day One. It has taken many years of growth to learn that the more I fully step into my divine feminine energy, the easier my work feels and the more valuable I become. I have always been a highly spiritual, deeply intuitive being that finds joy in connecting with the things we do not see. This part of me, my divine feminine, has been hidden away from my career world for fear of being called crazy, woo-woo, or "out there". The more fully I use my divine masculine and feminine gifts, the more balance I create, resulting in more success and abundance.

CHAPTER 11

Becoming a Servant Leader

"The best leaders are servant leaders. They serve those they lead."
Tony Hseih

The philosophy of servant leadership places the leader in the role of serving rather than simply directing. For centuries, people reporting to the leader have been the servants, working hard and looking for approval. In some cases, the leader has been an ego-based position, often based on title rather than ability.

Clearly, things have changed significantly as we collectively grow in consciousness. The great leader understands that if they serve as a coach whose primary focus is to create vision, set expectations, recognize wins, and remove obstacles, the sum of the team will achieve great things, making the leader's job easier.

Let me clarify one very important thing here. Servant leadership is not martyrdom. A martyr tries to take everything on themselves. They justify their behaviour as protecting those they serve by not delegating. They satisfy their ego by feeling like only they can do things right. Not only does this lead to burn out, but these actions send the message "I do not trust you" which leads to a decrease in engagement and motivation.

Part of being a servant leader is providing opportunities for others to grow, learn, and be in the spotlight for their contributions and wins. It is also important for the servant leader to support and understand when mistakes happen as this is an essential part of the growth process. Patience is a key virtue when it comes to servant leadership.

The conscious concept of servant leadership places the leader in the role of serving those around them rather than simply directing or instructing. It is a much more supportive and collaborative approach that enables team members to develop their careers rather than to simply execute tasks for the company. Employees who work for servant leaders tend to be much more highly engaged and, as a result, more efficient and effective.

Understanding Those You Serve

The move to this more inclusive style of leadership is necessary as the new generations need to feel a part of the team and to understand the vision. They need to work on purposeful projects and tasks rather than just coming to work to get a paycheque. These emerging generations are more interested in experiences than things. The Baby Boomers and even Generation X lived in a world where they could earn enough to buy a home. They found purpose and meaning in creating security and raising their families in traditional ways. However, as the cost of living has increased significantly, many younger adults wonder if they will ever be able to own a traditional family home. With greater access to the global world through the Internet, the younger generations are looking to experience life through expansive experiences and not by accumulating wealth and possessions in the traditional way.

Conscious leaders take these motivators into consideration when leading and creating workplace structures that support all of the generations in the workplace. I have heard some say, "Well, we can't make it about them. We have a business to run." My answer to this way of thinking is simple — if you need humans to achieve your business outcomes, you need to understand how to motivate those humans, otherwise you will be spending all of your time and money recruiting and training. This process will leave you feeling not only frustrated but burnt out. In order to access momentum, you need to understand your people and what motivates them to be efficient and aligned. A servant leader knows their people, knows what motivates them, sets the vision, explains why it is important and how it will positively impact everyone on the team, and then simply removes any obstacles or barriers for their team members.

Servant leadership is definitely the way to optimize success in our modern business climate made up of emerging generations; however, in order to make this conscious form of leadership sustainable and not have negative personal impacts, we need to first and foremost take care of the servant leader.

Servant leadership can only truly begin when the leader has ascended to a certain point of consciousness by healing core wounds and triggers. Once we heal the foundational wounds that block our lower energy centres, we can truly and authentically lead from our heart space with ease. We are then able to step into a place of servant leadership.

A Path to Conscious Leadership

Most often when you learn about leadership, the focus is on the skills you need to develop to be a great leader, and these are indeed very important; however, without also focusing on the areas you need to heal or balance first, you will always struggle. When we focus on removing the obstacles and creating balance within ourselves first, we can then naturally excel in the key areas of leadership success.

In my experience working with many incredible leaders, I have come to learn that servant leadership is a concept that many aspire to implement. They are out there serving, giving, and producing; however, something is off. Frustration and resentment build. Servant leaders feel unappreciated or unseen, possibly even taken for granted. They are giving until it hurts — either through exhaustion, burnout, or the emotional sadness of not being viewed as the committed contributor they are.

This happens when we serve from an unhealed place such as when we are serving for the purpose of receiving something in exchange or proving our own worth. In this case, the concept of servant leadership is not sustainable and will only lead to a place of frustration and eventually poor performance. However, when we serve from a whole place because we have done the work and healed our own wounds, we are giving not to receive something in return but simply to serve.

In Chapter 6 - You Are Energy, you learned about the chakras and what emotions create an imbalance within each of them. Now we are going to use the chakras as a pathway to support you in becoming a more balanced and conscious leader.

Let's begin by looking at the path to balanced conscious leadership, starting with your root chakra at the base of your spine and seeing how it unfolds as we move upwards.

Root Chakra	Create foundations and feel safe and secure. Release fear and sadness.
Sacral Chakra	Invite in creativity, ease, and flow. Release guilt and shame.
Solar Plexus Chakra	Be authentic and build trust. Release self-doubt and a lack of trust that everything is and will work out in your highest and best good.
Heart Chakra	Become a servant leader. Release the need to be a people pleaser or overachiever to gain acceptance. Stand in a place of high value and worth. Display balanced emotions. Release a lack of self-worth.
Throat Chakra	Become an effective communicator and use your voice in an effective way to influence. Release the fear of what will happen if you speak your truth.
Third Eye Chakra	Trust your intuition. Be aligned to your divine guidance. Release overthinking, questioning, and doubting yourself.
Crown Chakra	Believe you are fully supported and aligned to something powerful. Release the feeling of being alone or the need to be completely independent in order to be successful or valuable.

Now that you understand the pathway and how creating balance within each of your energy centres will remove obstacles and align you with core abilities that will skyrocket your success, let's take a closer look at each chakra and discover and heal any imbalances that may be currently present.

Create Foundations - Balance Your Root Chakra

Your success and happiness are built upon foundations created by balancing the root chakra (the primary chakra) which is engaged at birth and involves our emotional and mental health. Our desire for logic, order, and structure all stem from our root chakra. It carries the energetic belief that we are all connected and that the choices we make as well as how we treat one another directly influence the whole.

The root chakra has to do with being comfortable with one's own being as well as connecting to the earth and community. When your root chakra is flowing freely, you feel like you belong and are supported in every way. You have family and friends who are always there for you, and you are financially secure. It's all about feeling grounded, safe, and secure.

When you have a blocked root chakra, you experience a feeling of not belonging. You may struggle with your finances, relationships, self-esteem, and body issues. You likely neglect your body and its basic needs. Difficulties with your family leave you feeling unsupported, anxious, and alone. You will likely be unfulfilled in your career, feeling like you're not doing what you are meant to be doing. Some also struggle with paranoia, aggression, or mania.

When your root chakra is overactive, your survival needs become an obsession. You may be either extremely insecure or manipulative and controlling. You likely have issues with being an overachiever and a people pleaser. An addiction to drugs, food, money, alcohol, or gambling is often present with an overactive root chakra.

Answer the following questions to see if you may have an imbalance in your root chakra:

1. In what areas of your life do you feel unsafe?

2. Are there some areas in your life where you feel like there is never enough?

3. In what areas of your life do you feel like you have no control or power to make a choice?

4. Are there any areas of your life where you are missing healthy boundaries?

5. Do you trust that life supports you?

6. Do you make decisions that are healthy and support you?

7. Do you struggle to make a decision?

What did these questions uncover for you? If you are uncertain, ask your subconscious mind to bring forward into your awareness anything that may be creating imbalance in your root chakra.

Use the root chakra chart below to help identify if you have any imbalances in this energy centre and to discover ways to heal and regain balance so you can begin to thrive.

Creating Foundations - Balancing the Root Chakra

When in Balance	You feel like you belong and are supported in every way. Friends and family are always there to support you. You feel grounded, safe, and secure.
Signs of Imbalance	You feel like you do not belong, or you have financial struggles, relationship problems, self-esteem, and body issues. You feel unsupported, anxious, or alone. You might not feel fulfilled in your career or that you are doing what you are meant to do. If overactive: Survival or finances become your obsession. You are extremely insecure, manipulative, or controlling, an overachiever or people pleaser. You may have an addiction to food, alcohol, money, or gambling.
Physical Manifestations	Anxiety disorders, nightmares, fears, issues with colon, lower back, bladder, lower legs, feet, prostate issues in men, cancer, varicose veins, depression, immune-related disorders
Ask Yourself	What are you most afraid of? Write it on a piece of paper and burn it in a safe, contained space to transmute the energy and let it go.
Release	Fear
Affirmations	"I am safe." "I trust in the process of life." "I love my body and am grateful it supports me." "I am creating solid foundations."
Do These Things	Wear red, walk in nature, feel the earth under your feet. Smell the trees, nature, and the ocean.
Use These Gemstones	Amber and agate
Eat These Foods	Red meat, animal fat, spinach, hot peppers (unless overactive then decrease consumption)
Play Music Which	Vibrates to C note
Meditations	You can easily find free root chakra meditations or healing music on YouTube. Switch between root chakra and overall (all 7) chakra healing meditations for optimal results.
Expedite The Process	Work with a coach, an energy healer, reiki, or other spiritual practitioner to help you unlock your blocks.

Be Creative - Balance Your Sacral Chakra

The second or sacral chakra is represented by the colour orange and seeks to create relationships for your physical survival. It is extremely volatile as it links to sex, power, and money. It is where your sense of personal identity resides and provides the awareness that self-protection and preservation are important. Balancing the sacral chakra will help us understand that we can't control others and that the conflict we create in our relationships is a reflection of how we feel about ourselves.

The creative energy held within the sacral chakra will serve you well. Without this energy, your behaviour, thoughts, and relationships may become stagnant. Boredom will begin to set in. Balancing the sacral chakra helps you break out of the same old habits and helps you learn and grow.

When you have a blocked sacral chakra, relationships are a constant struggle and a source of great pain. You will feel like you lack creativity to express yourself, and you will likely have a low sex drive. You may also have a tendency towards self-destruction and self-abuse. A common indicator of a damaged sacral chakra is equating being loved to being desired sexually. Dysfunctional relationships are often repeated over and over, and you may start to feel numb towards others. Some people with a blocked sacral chakra will think that sex is evil, wrong, or shameful. It's also important to note here that gossip and manipulation weaken the sacral chakra.

If your sacral chakra is overactive, you may be a workaholic or a person who pursues pleasure to the point of being greedy. You likely have a domineering energy which comes across as too intense for most people. Many people with an overactive sacral chakra use addictions to food, sex, pornography, drugs, or alcohol as a substitute for love. Another indicator of an overactive sacral chakra is having many projects going at the same time but never completing any of them.

Answer the following questions to you see if you have an imbalance in your sacral chakra:

1. In what areas of your life do you feel withdrawn or like you are holding back?

2. Do you ever feel like you lack courage or feel hopeless?

3. Where in your life do you feel obligated rather than inspired to do something?

4. Are you relying on someone else for something but are afraid you might not receive it?

5. Are you dependent on someone for your financial or emotional needs?

6. Do you give yourself the freedom to be yourself?

7. Do you ever feel resentful about what others expect from you?

Did these questions bring up anything that might indicate an unbalanced sacral chakra? If you are uncertain, ask your subconscious mind to bring forward into your awareness anything that may be a block on this chakra.

Use the sacral chakra chart below to help identify if you have any imbalances in this energy centre and to discover ways to heal and regain balance so you can begin to thrive.

Be Creative - Balancing the Sacral Chakra

When in Balance	You feel like you are cherished and special. You are free from enemies. You are eloquent, and creativity flows through you. You have a healthy and passionate desire for sex.
Signs of Imbalance	You have an inability to express or feel emotion, you feel unhappy or insecure, you have attachment issues or sexually related guilt, you are timid or act cold towards others. If overactive: You experience emotional volatility, hypersensitivity, trust issues, or act needy or emotionally dependent.
Physical Manifestations	Sharp pain, ache, tingle or sensitivity in the lower abdomen, lower back ache, pre-menstrual syndrome, uterine fibroids, ovarian cysts, IBS, endometriosis, testicular disease, prostatic disease
Ask Yourself	What am I blaming myself for? Write it on a piece of paper and burn it in a safe, contained space to transmute the energy and let it go.
Release	Guilt
Affirmations	"I am a creative and sensual being." "I am a talented, creative being." "I love feeling pleasure in my body." "I am surrounded by relationships that feel good." "I am creating a fabulous life with beautiful and loving relationships."
Do These Things	Wear orange. Dance or do hip-opening yoga poses. Aromatherapy: clary sage, jasmine, rose, ylang ylang, and sandalwood oils
Use These Gemstones	Carnelian, amber, and orange calcite
Eat These Foods	Honey, almonds, cinnamon, strawberries, melon, and coconut. If overactive, eat less of these.
Play Music Which	Vibrates to D note
Meditations	You can easily find free sacral chakra meditations or healing music on YouTube. Switch between sacral chakra and overall (all 7) chakra healing meditations for optimal results.
Expedite The Process	Work with a coach, an energy healer, reiki, or other spiritual practitioner to help you unlock your blocks.

Be Authentic - Balance Your Solar Plexus Chakra

Authenticity comes with ease when the solar plexus chakra is balanced. The solar plexus is the third chakra and is represented by the colour yellow. It is where the fight or flight mechanism lives energetically. We "take flight" when the solar plexus chakra is blocked, and we "fight" when it is overactive. Depending on whether our chakras are blocked or overactive will give us different experiences, especially when it comes to the solar plexus chakra.

It is common for the solar plexus chakra to be weaker in new settings or around people we don't feel comfortable with, and it can shine brightly around our close friends or in settings we've grown accustomed to and can naturally be ourselves.

When you have a blocked solar plexus chakra, you feel disempowered and have lower self-esteem. This is where we energetically see the victim mentality. You become oversensitive to criticism and may fear looking foolish. You struggle to make healthy decisions due to a low opinion of yourself. You may tend to avoid confrontation and are unable to advocate for yourself. Other symptoms of a blocked solar plexus chakra include being overly cautious or naïve, having difficulty concentrating, feeling lethargic, and often refusing to accept responsibility for one's own actions.

When the solar plexus chakra is overactive, you have a fear of failure and can be aggressive. Some people use the power of their solar plexus to keep their hearts closed to avoid emotional pain. This affects relationships and decision-making. It can be difficult to make friends and sustain relationships when you have an overactive solar plexus chakra because you can be narrow-minded and overly critical of others.

Answer the following questions to see if you have an imbalance in your solar plexus chakra:

1. Do you trust your instincts, or do you find yourself often relying on others for advice?

2. Can you recall a time when you found yourself avoiding a strong or confident person?

3. Do you avoid or find it difficult to make decisions? Has this happened in the past few months?

4. Have you avoided doing or saying something because you are afraid others will judge or criticize you?

5. Do you often compare yourself to others? When you do, what do you say about yourself?

6. Are you saying to yourself, "I will do it when I earn my next degree, lose that last ten pounds, make more money, or have the right person in my life?"

7. Where in your life are you afraid to fail?

Did these questions bring up anything that might indicate an unbalanced solar plexus chakra? If you are uncertain, ask your subconscious mind to bring forward into your awareness anything that may be creating imbalance in this chakra.

Use the solar plexus chakra chart below to help identify if you have any imbalances in this energy centre and to discover ways to heal and regain balance so you can begin to thrive.

Be Authentic - Balancing the Solar Plexus Chakra

When in Balance	You will experience intense and positive personal power allowing you to create the life you desire. You will have the ability to make your dreams come true.
Signs of Imbalance	You might feel disempowered or lethargic, have low self-esteem, suffer from victim mentality, fear looking foolish, be overly sensitive to criticism or overly cautious, have difficulty making healthy choices, accepting responsibility for your actions, or concentrating, or avoid confrontation. If overactive: you feel like life is a fight, you fear failure, you are sometimes aggressive and may be narrow-minded or critical of others.
Physical Manifestations	Digestive issues, liver problems, adrenal dysfunction, arthritis, eating disorders
Ask Yourself	What am I ashamed about? Write it on a piece of paper and burn it in a safe, contained space to transmute the energy and let it go.
Release	Shame
Affirmations	"I am powerful." "I am using my power to make a positive difference." "I easily manifest my desires." "I trust my own guidance." "I am a powerful creator of my life." "I am authentic."
Do These Things	Wear yellow, breathe into your abdomen, and then smile and spend time in the sun.
Use These Gemstones	Topaz and citrine
Eat These Foods	Starches, carrots, apples, apricots, squash, chicken, and fish or less of each if overactive
Play Music Which	Vibrates to E note
Meditations	You can easily find free solar plexus chakra meditations or healing music on YouTube. Switch between solar plexus chakra and overall (all 7) chakra healing meditations for optimal results.
Expedite The Process	Work with a coach, an energy healer, reiki or other spiritual practitioner to help you unlock your blocks.

Connection - Balance Your Heart Chakra

The heart or fourth chakra is one of the most powerful chakras, originating in the middle of the chest and resting at the centre of the human energy system. It is represented by the colour green or light pink. Many people believe they can suffer from a broken heart, but in truth, emotional pain causes our hearts to close or become blocked which gives the feeling of being broken. This chakra connects us to the greatest power on earth, love. It allows us to give and receive love unconditionally.

When your heart chakra is flowing freely, you are not only compassionate but grateful for the life you've been given. The lesson of this chakra is that we must love ourselves and realize our self-worth before we can truly love and fully receive love from another. When your heart chakra is balanced, you do not need to jump from one job or relationship to the next; waiting for the "right one" suits you just fine.

When you have a blocked heart chakra, you fear commitment, believe you must please others to receive love, and feel like you must protect yourself from being hurt. You have issues with trust which leaves you isolated and lonely. You can become quite needy, jealous, bossy, pessimistic, and greedy. A blocked heart chakra makes you incapable of loving yourself so you feel you must change in some way to be loved. You are also closed off to forgiveness, and this bitterness makes you blame others for your current situation.

When your heart chakra is overactive, you have difficulty taking control of your emotions. You fear that people will judge and be critical of you, just as you are of them. Your love is conditional; you are only able to love people if they meet your standards. When you are in a relationship that is not serving you well, you often have trouble walking away.

Answer the following questions to see if there is an imbalance in your heart chakra:

1. What is the most significant loss in your life? At what age do you recall first experiencing grief?

2. Have you suffered from a breakup, divorce, or other relationship loss?

3. Is there someone in your life that has hurt you so deeply you are finding it difficult to forgive them?

4. When you think about love, are you ever afraid of being hurt?

5. Can you think about a time when you changed the way you thought, behaved, dressed, or ate to be "more lovable"?

6. Have you experienced a chest cold, bronchitis, or pneumonia in the last two years?

7. Do you seem to attract people who have a fear of commitment, or do you think you may have a fear of commitment?

Did these questions bring up anything that might indicate an unbalanced heart chakra? If you are uncertain, ask your subconscious mind to bring forward into your awareness anything that may be blocking this chakra.

Use the heart chakra chart below to help identify if you have any imbalances in this energy centre and to discover ways to heal and regain balance so you can begin to thrive.

Connection - Balancing the Heart Chakra

When in Balance	You feel compassionate and grateful. You do not have to jump from one job or relationship to the next; you are content waiting for the right one. You have healed and let go of your emotional wounds.
Signs of Imbalance	You might have a fear of commitment. You might feel like you must please others to receive love or protect yourself from being hurt. You might have trust issues, feel isolated, lonely, needy, bossy, jealous, pessimistic, or greedy. When your heart is blocked, it is not possible to love yourself, so you feel you need to change somehow to be loved. If overactive: You might have difficulty taking control of your emotions, you fear judgement and criticism as you tend to be judgemental and critical, your love is conditional, and you have trouble walking away from relationships that do not serve you.
Physical Manifestations	Congestive heart failure, heart attack, mitral valve prolapses, asthma, lung or breast cancer, pain in ribs especially on the right side of the body. Respiration or circulatory problems, bronchitis, pneumonia, cold hands or feet
Ask Yourself	What am I sad about? Write it on a piece of paper and burn it in a safe, contained space to transmute the energy and let it go.
Release	Grief
Affirmations	"I am love." "I completely love and accept myself." "It is easy to feel compassion for others." "I accept myself and others easily." "I allow love to flow to me with ease." "Love is abundant in my world."
Do These Things	Straighten your back and lift your chest as you pull your shoulders back. Spend time with a baby or toddler and feel their love. Wear green or pink. Look in the mirror and say, "I love you". Listen to a loved one's heartbeat and then have them listen to yours. Breathe in some fresh air. Massage your hands or have someone else do it. Use lavender aromatherapy as it calms the nervous system.
Use These Gemstones	Emerald and rose quartz
Eat These Foods	Strawberries, cherries, brown rice, and vegetables or less of these if overactive
Play Music Which	Vibrates to F note
Meditations	You can easily find free heart chakra meditations or healing music on YouTube. Switch between heart chakra and overall (all 7) chakra healing meditations for optimal results.
Expedite The Process	Work with a coach, an energy healer, reiki, or other spiritual practitioner to help you unlock your blocks.

Communicate Effectively - Balance Your Throat Chakra

Effective communication comes with more ease when the throat chakra is balanced. This fifth chakra is represented by the colour blue or indigo. It is responsible for communication, self-expression, and the ability to speak your personal truth.

A balanced throat chakra helps you communicate with clarity, wisdom, and discernment. When your throat chakra is in balance, you will find that you are not only able to speak fearlessly and with compassion, but you will also be open to listening to and hearing others. You will be able to articulate your ideas, feelings, and opinions clearly. By expressing your thoughts with clarity, you will find that you also feel heard and understood.

When you have a blocked throat chakra, you tend to be fearful about speaking your personal truth, find it more difficult to express your thoughts, or feel anxious about speaking or communicating. You may have really good ideas, but your fear of being judged prevents you from sharing them.

When your throat chakra is overactive, you often talk in excess. You may suffer from a stutter. You may have an inability to listen, like to gossip, have a loud or dominating voice, or tend to interrupt. You may be highly opinionated and critical.

Answer the following questions to see if there is an imbalance in your throat chakra:

1. Do you ever feel afraid to share ideas or thoughts in meetings or with friends?

2. Do you only speak if spoken to?

3. Do you notice that you tend to interrupt often?

4. Have you ever noticed that you slightly raise your voice in a conversation in order to continue speaking?

5. Do you struggle to remember the details of what others have shared in conversation?

6. Has anyone told you that you could improve your listening skills?

7. Do you often suffer from sore throats?

Did these questions bring up anything that might indicate an unbalanced throat chakra? If you are uncertain, ask your subconscious mind to bring forward into your awareness anything that may be blocking this chakra.

Use the throat chakra chart below to help you identify any imbalances in this energy centre and discover how to heal and create balance so you can begin to thrive.

Communicate Effectively - Balancing the Throat Chakra

When in Balance	You feel like you can communicate with clarity, wisdom, and discernment. You are able to speak fearlessly and with compassion. Your communication style enables you to influence others, and you feel heard and understood.
Signs of Imbalance	You fear speaking your truth, struggle to express yourself, or feel very anxious when you have to communicate your thoughts or ideas. You fear being judged if you communicate. You have a stutter or a tendency to interrupt. You are unable to listen or are overly opinionated and critical.
Physical Manifestations	A raspy throat, chronic sore throat, mouth ulcers, gum disease, laryngitis, thyroid challenges, temporomandibular joint (TMJ) disorders
Ask Yourself	Am I afraid to speak and share my ideas? Do I feel like I will be judged for speaking my truth? Do I try to control conversations? Do I often interrupt conversations to get my point across?
Release	The fear of what will happen if you speak your truth
Affirmations	"I speak with clarity and compassion." "I am a good communicator." "I listen to understand." "It is safe to speak my truth."
Do These Things	Wear blue or surround yourself with the colour blue, do neck stretches or breathing exercises, journal, try yoga poses (Shoulder Stand, Plow, Fish), chant the seed sound "Ham," and keep your neck aligned with your spine.
Use These Gemstones	Amazonite and lapis lazuli
Eat These Foods	Drink plenty of water and warm herbal teas. Eat nuts and seeds, blueberries, plums, aubergine, purple grapes, purple cabbage, purple carrots, and goji berries.
Play Music Which	Vibrates to G note
Meditations	You can easily find free throat chakra meditations or healing music on YouTube. Switch between throat chakra and overall (all 7) chakra healing meditations for optimal results.
Expedite The Process	Work with a coach, an energy healer, reiki, or other spiritual practitioner to help you unlock your blocks.

See Clearly - Balance Your Third Eye Chakra

Having a clear vision and knowing the next steps to take comes with ease when the third eye chakra is balanced. The sixth chakra is located in the centre of your head in between your eyebrows. It is represented by the colour purple. It is linked to perception, awareness, clarity, concentration, and imagination.

A balanced third eye chakra enables you to see the true, unified world, whereas the physical eyes only perceive the limited physical world. When in balance, you have mental clarity, improved concentration, clear self-expression, strengthened intuition, strong insights, the ability to be decisive, and a sense of bliss.

When you have a blocked third eye chakra, you feel a sense of confusion or uncertainty, and you may suffer from cynicism, pessimism, and a lack of purpose.

When your third eye chakra is overactive, you may have hallucinations or suffer from paranoia, delusions, or mental fog, be judgemental, or feel overwhelmed or anxious.

Answer the following questions to see if there is an imbalance in your third eye chakra:

1. Do you struggle to make decisions?

2. Is it challenging for you to focus on tasks and complete goals?

3. Do you feel like you have a lack of direction and no idea how to shift it?

4. Do you find yourself often focused on the things that are going wrong?

5. Do you suffer from headaches, sinus problems, or insomnia?

Did these questions bring up anything that might indicate an unbalanced third eye chakra? If you are uncertain, ask your subconscious mind to bring forward into your awareness anything that may be blocking this chakra.

Use the third eye chakra chart below to help you identify any imbalances in this energy centre and discover how to heal and create balance so you can begin to thrive.

Seeing Clearly - Balancing the Third Eye Chakra

When in Balance	It's easy for you to develop a clear vision and know what steps to take to achieve it. You have mental clarity, good concentration, clear self-expression, strengthened intuition, strong insights, the ability to be decisive, and a sense of bliss. You see the world as united rather than divided.
Signs of Imbalance	You feel a sense of confusion or uncertainty, and you may suffer from cynicism, pessimism, and a lack of purpose. You experience hallucinations, paranoia, delusions, or mental fog. You are judgemental or feel overwhelmed or anxious.
Physical Manifestations	Headaches, vision problems, seizures, insomnia, nausea, sinus issues
Ask Yourself	Do I often feel confused? Do I struggle with knowing what is the right action to take? Do I struggle to stay focused and on task? Do I doubt myself and my actions?
Release	The fear of not knowing how things will unfold
Affirmations	"I trust my intuition always." "I trust my highest good is unfolding." "I see all things clearly." "My intuition knows the way."
Do These Things	Wear or surround yourself with indigo or purple, do yoga, meditate, pray, dance, chant the OM sound.
Use These Gemstones	Amethyst, clear quartz, purple fluorite, and lapis lazuli
Eat These Foods	Raw cacao, goji berries, garlic, lemon, watermelon, star anise, honey, or coconut oil
Play Music Which	Vibrates to A note
Meditations	You can easily find free third eye chakra meditations or healing music on YouTube. Switch between third eye chakra and overall (all 7) chakra healing meditations for optimal results.
Expedite The Process	Work with a coach, an energy healer, reiki, or other spiritual practitioner to help you unlock your blocks.

Feeling Connected – Balance Your Crown Chakra

Feeling connected to something outside of yourself and knowing that you are never alone in the path to your ultimate success and highest potential is the result of a balanced crown chakra. The crown chakra is the seventh chakra and is located at the top of the head. It is usually represented by the colour white, gold, or violet. The crown chakra is responsible for our inner and outer beauty and our spiritual connection. Interestingly, it is said that the crown chakra does not develop until between the ages of 43 – 49.

A balanced crown chakra provides us with the spiritual awareness that we are connected to something bigger than ourselves. As Erica Matluck, ND, describes it, "It allows us to put our short-sighted self-interests aside in service of the whole, transcending victimhood and isolation with trust and purpose." When our crown chakra is balanced, we feel connected to the universe, the earth, and people, we are peaceful, we have good mental clarity, we sleep well, and we experience acceptance. We are on a path of enlightenment.

When you have a blocked crown chakra, you feel isolated, disconnected, and out of touch with anything beyond yourself. While mental health is affected by a variety of biological, social, and environmental factors, spiritual well-being is integral. An imbalanced crown chakra leads to insomnia, hypersomnia, rigid thoughts, analysis paralysis, fear of alienation, poor balance and coordination, an attachment to material things, and a sense of being ungrounded.

When your crown chakra is overactive you may experience recurring headaches or sensitivity to light and sound. Emotionally, you may lack empathy. You may be caught in a cycle of addiction or living in a fantasy. You may have rigid religious beliefs or feel a sense of superiority over others.

Answer the following questions to see if there is an imbalance in your crown chakra:

1. Do you often feel alone or unsupported?

2. Have you been told that you are rigid in your beliefs?

3. Do you often feel like you are better than most people around you?

4. Do you have problems sleeping?

5. Do you have trust issues?

Did these questions bring up anything that might indicate an unbalanced crown chakra? If you are uncertain, ask your subconscious mind to bring forward into your awareness anything that may be blocking this chakra.

Use the crown chakra chart below to help identify if you have any imbalances in this energy centre and to discover ways to heal and regain balance so you can begin to thrive.

Feeling Connected - Balancing the Crown Chakra

When in Balance	You feel like you are connected to and supported by something bigger. You trust in the natural process of life and its divine timing. You seek unity and look for similarities as you understand all people are connected. You feel happy and at times even blissful. You are open-minded, thoughtful, intelligent, and aware.
Signs of Imbalance	You may experience feelings of isolation, disconnection, and depression. Alternatively, you feel superior to most people and are very judgemental. You lack empathy, fear alienation, suffer from poor balance and coordination, and do not feel grounded or supported. You have rigid religious beliefs or ideas.
Physical Manifestations	Headaches, sensitivity to light and sounds, insomnia, hypersomnia, poor balance, and coordination
Ask Yourself	Do I feel alienated or disconnected? Do I have rigid beliefs? Am I lacking in trust that life will work out in my highest and best good?
Release	The need to be completely independent to be valuable
Affirmations	"I am divinely inspired, guided, and protected." "I am open-minded." "The universe has my back." "I surrender and trust in infinite possibilities."
Do These Things	Be quiet, meditate, wear white, gold or lavender, do yoga, practise spirituality in whatever form that most resonates with you. Do acts of kindness. Be empathetic. Surrender.
Use These Gemstones	Clear quartz
Eat These Foods	Mushrooms, garlic, ginger, onion, lychee, and coconut
Play Music Which	Vibrates to B note
Meditations	You can easily find free crown chakra meditations or healing music on YouTube. Switch between crown chakra and overall (all 7) chakra healing meditations for optimal results.
Expedite The Process	Work with a coach, an energy healer, reiki, or other spiritual practitioner to help you unlock your blocks.

When you do an assessment of what is blocking your energy centres and bring them into balance and alignment, you will naturally begin to feel much lighter and more confident. When you are in a state of ease, that which is surrounding you becomes easy. Remember, everything is energy and when you are balanced, your overall frequency elevates which allows you to be open and receive all the goodness that life has to offer you.

CHAPTER 12

Boundaries and Needs

"You are not required to set yourself on fire to keep others warm."
Unknown

We have now spent a fair amount of time working on identifying, clearing, and balancing things that may have been limiting your potential by affecting the way you show up in certain situations and relationships.

In order to ensure that the work you have done is not lost or absorbed by other experiences moving forward, we must now define your needs, establish boundaries, and learn how to positively communicate them so that you can proactively protect yourself and continue to support your new level of conscious behaviours that are enabling you to flourish.

Before we start to define your needs, let's talk a little bit about boundaries.

Boundaries are very in vogue these days. "Boundary" has become somewhat of a buzz word as we grow in universal consciousness. We know we need them, but it might end there. We may even set an intention to have boundaries. However, without a clear process of understanding our needs, defining where we may need a boundary, and how thoughtful communication can support it, we might not get very far. We might slip back into our unconscious patterns of people pleasing and over-achieving, leading us back to burnout, struggle, and unfulfilment.

Why do we struggle to set boundaries? There are many reasons. First and foremost, we have convinced ourselves that having needs means we are "needy". Being needy will result in a negative response from those we interact with. We fear that a negative response equals others not liking us which will result in the loss of connection, respect, or love we deeply crave as human beings.

In our pursuit of connection, we push our needs aside. The thing is our needs do not go away — they simply lie there unmet in the shadows. When our needs are not met, we feel unfulfilled, and over time, this can lead to negative emotions like unhappiness and resentment. Therefore, defining our needs and understanding where we may need to communicate a boundary to support these needs is one of the most positive things you can do to take care of yourself. Remember, taking care of yourself is the first step in becoming a servant leader as you cannot serve others if your cup is not full.

Stanford Education says, "Boundaries help determine what is and is not okay in a relationship — whether that be with friends, partners, co-workers, bosses, or family members. Ideally, we put them in place to protect our well-being. They help us to build trust, safety, and respect in relationships. Common boundaries include emotional, physical, sexual, intellectual, and financial; they can apply to any aspect of your life where you feel they are needed." [Source – Stanford Student Affairs]

But we struggle to define and implement boundaries, don't we? I believe it starts with the word itself — **boundary** — it has a strong somewhat off-putting energy to it. This is challenging as the people who suffer from not having boundaries are likely the ones who take a step back from this strong word, making it even more difficult for them to protect themselves. Or those who are naturally more confident may attempt to come charging in demanding their boundaries be respected. Neither works well.

When you think of the word boundary, what comes to mind? Is it a solid grey wall or a soft pink or green energetic light? Can you feel the difference? If we think of the former, we think of setting boundaries as somewhat offensive and certainly not very polite. As caring, conscious people, we are sensitive to how we make others feel. It is a good thing to not want to come across as demanding or self-centred; however, failure to have and positively communicate your boundaries can be harmful.

The failure to create and communicate our boundaries will keep us in a cycle of not getting our needs met which will eventually lead to negative behaviours and responses. Resentment starts to build, and we exhibit negative, passive-aggressive behaviours that come across poorly to others; we risk everything we were hoping to achieve by not having boundaries in the first place.

Having boundaries is an act of self-care. They are essential for you to maintain balance, success, and happiness in your life.

But before we can identify what boundaries we need to set in place, we must understand our needs. Our needs are much more than our desires. They are the baseline of what we require in order to truly be happy and fulfilled in our lives. They are the components that, if sacrificed, will eventually cause us harm.

The needs assessment that follows is an excellent tool for understanding your needs. I know you will benefit from the self-awareness this exercise will bring.

UNDERSTANDING YOUR NEEDS

Understanding your needs is a very powerful tool for self-awareness. We often speak about our wants and/or desires, but if our needs are not met, we are not able to move beyond that. Personally, knowing your needs enables you to ensure you are doing what is necessary to meet them. It also enables you to decrease frustration and unhappiness and better communicate your needs to the key people you interact with in life. This is an excellent tool for empowerment. In order to complete the assessment, you can either complete it here in your book or alternatively, go to https://glowleadership.com/needs to complete an online version or to download a paper copy. Additionally, you can flip to the back of this book to activate the QR Code.

Definitions:

Needs are conditions, things, and feelings that you must have to be minimally satisfied in life. Often, needs are the things that must be met before you can really "get on" with life. When you have unmet needs, you are usually "bound" or "hooked" by people, events, and thoughts; you are more susceptible to being sad, depressed, angry, or resentful. Remember, needs are what you must have, not what you want, prefer, or deserve.

Wants are distinct from needs and represent conditions, things, or experiences that you feel like you want to have to feel better about yourself, your life, etc. Wants come from past experiences, your upbringing, advertising, or unmet needs. When your needs are met, you find that your want list has less of a pull on you. Remember, wants are what you want to have but could actually live without.

PART ONE – NEEDS ASSESSMENT

In Part One of the Needs Assessment, go through each of the following sections and the statements in them and select whether you:

1. Strongly Agree

2. Agree

3. Neutral

4. Disagree

5. Strongly Disagree

SECTION 1

1 2 3 4 5   1. I need acceptance from most everyone.

1 2 3 4 5   2. I need acceptance from my family.

1 2 3 4 5   3. I need acceptance from a particular person.

1 2 3 4 5   4. I have a very hard time if am not included in a conversation or event.

1 2 3 4 5   5. I have a very hard time if I don't perceive I am being accepted.

SECTION 2

1 2 3 4 5   1. I need to accomplish great things during my lifetime.

1 2 3 4 5   2. I need to accomplish something during my lifetime.

1 2 3 4 5   3. I need to almost always be engaged in accomplishing something.

1 2 3 4 5   4. I have a very hard time just relaxing and doing nothing for weeks.

1 2 3 4 5   5. I have a very hard time if I am not accomplishing something big.

SECTION 3

1 2 3 4 5   1. I need to be acknowledged by most everyone that I help or work with.

1 2 3 4 5   2. I need to be acknowledged or complimented when I look good.

1 2 3 4 5   3. I need to be acknowledged by only one or just a few close friends.

1 2 3 4 5   4. I have a very hard time receiving criticism without some added praise.

1 2 3 4 5   5. I have a very hard time if I do not get acknowledged regularly.

SECTION 4

1 2 3 4 5	1. I need to be loved by many people.
1 2 3 4 5	2. I need to be loved by a close circle of friends.
1 2 3 4 5	3. I need to be loved by one particular person.
1 2 3 4 5	4. I have a very hard time if I do not feel an important person loves me.
1 2 3 4 5	5. I have a very hard time if I don't feel loved enough.

SECTION 5

1 2 3 4 5	1. I need to be accurate or right in most situations.
1 2 3 4 5	2. I need to be accurate or right in my area of expertise.
1 2 3 4 5	3. I need to be accurate or right all of the time.
1 2 3 4 5	4. If I am mistaken about something, I take it personally.
1 2 3 4 5	5. If I make a mistake, I take it personally and hard.

SECTION 6

1 2 3 4 5	1. I need to be cared for/loved by many people.
1 2 3 4 5	2. I need to be cared for/loved by a select group of people.
1 2 3 4 5	3. I need to be cared for/loved by one particular person.
1 2 3 4 5	4. When I don't feel cared for, I get resentful and even bitter.
1 2 3 4 5	5. If I don't feel cared for, I have a very hard time.

SECTION 7

1 2 3 4 5   1. I need what people say to be perfectly clear.

1 2 3 4 5   2. I need to be certain about what I am reading, hearing, or working on.

1 2 3 4 5   3. I need to be able to hear clearly what people are saying.

1 2 3 4 5   4. I have a very hard time if I am not clear about things important to me.

1 2 3 4 5   5. I have a very hard time if I am not certain about what's going on.

SECTION 8

1 2 3 4 5   1. I need a very comfortable bed in which to sleep.

1 2 3 4 5   2. I need the most comfortable job there is.

1 2 3 4 5   3. I need "all the comforts of home" when I travel.

1 2 3 4 5   4. If I know I may be uncomfortable somewhere, I may not go.

1 2 3 4 5   5. When I am uncomfortable, I am very grumpy or "put out".

SECTION 9

1 2 3 4 5   1. I need to say what's on my mind even if it's not always appropriate.

1 2 3 4 5   2. I need others to say what's on their mind even if they don't want to.

1 2 3 4 5   3. I need only the key people in my life to communicate with me fully.

1 2 3 4 5   4. When I hold back and don't speak my mind, I start losing energy.

1 2 3 4 5   5. When others don't fully communicate, I get upset or frightened.

SECTION 10

1 2 3 4 5   1. I need an option to stop things if they do not go the way I need them to.

1 2 3 4 5   2. I need to keep the upper hand in most situations.

1 2 3 4 5   3. I need to tell people what to do.

1 2 3 4 5   4. If others start telling me what to do, I react strongly.

1 2 3 4 5   5. If we can't do it my way, I'll likely leave or find people who will.

SECTION 11

1 2 3 4 5   1. I need to be the primary one that makes something happen.

1 2 3 4 5   2. I need to be the "critical link" in bringing two people together.

1 2 3 4 5   3. I need to be known as the person who gets projects done on time.

1 2 3 4 5   4. If I don't feel needed, I am very uncomfortable.

1 2 3 4 5   5. I feel left out when something good happens, and I am not a part of it.

SECTION 12

1 2 3 4 5   1. I need to do exactly what my duty is for my friends and family.

1 2 3 4 5   2. I need to do my duty to my job, clients, or employer.

1 2 3 4 5   3. I need to do my duty to my country and/or church.

1 2 3 4 5   4. If I can't do my duty as I see it, I feel "held back" or suppressed.

1 2 3 4 5   5. If my duty is not clear, I am uncomfortable.

SECTION 13

1 2 3 4 5   1. I need to feel physically unrestrained and free.

1 2 3 4 5   2. I need for my time to be my own.

1 2 3 4 5   3. I need for my thoughts, actions, and choices to be my own.

1 2 3 4 5   4. I feel trapped when I feel obligated or expected to do something.

1 2 3 4 5   5. I am unhappy when I do not have a sense that I am free from all things.

SECTION 14

1 2 3 4 5   1. I need everyone around me to tell the truth and not mislead or cheat.

1 2 3 4 5   2. I need my close friends to be honest with me and not "hold back".

1 2 3 4 5   3. I need to tell the truth all the time.

1 2 3 4 5   4. When someone lies to me and I find out, I get very upset.

1 2 3 4 5   5. When I have compromised my own integrity, I get very upset.

SECTION 15

1 2 3 4 5   1. I need things around me to be in their proper place or order.

1 2 3 4 5   2. I need/want to make my bed each day.

1 2 3 4 5   3. I need/want a specific plan of action so I know what I am doing.

1 2 3 4 5   4. When my things are out of place or messy, I don't like it at all.

1 2 3 4 5   5. When things are said or done illogically, I don't usually like it.

SECTION 16

1 2 3 4 5   1. I need quiet in my workspace.

1 2 3 4 5   2. I need quiet at home.

1 2 3 4 5   3. I need to protect my sense of equilibrium and inner peace.

1 2 3 4 5   4. I lose my sense of security being in noise or commotion for too long.

1 2 3 4 5   5. When I lose my sense of self, I have to go to a quiet space to regain it.

SECTION 17

1 2 3 4 5   1. I need the absolute ability and opportunity to get what I want in life.

1 2 3 4 5   2. I need all the power I can get.

1 2 3 4 5   3. I need the opportunity to change the course of things.

1 2 3 4 5   4. When I feel powerless, it's extremely frustrating.

1 2 3 4 5   5. I feel lost when I have no one around me to manage or impact.

SECTION 18

1 2 3 4 5   1. I need to be recognized for what I've done.

1 2 3 4 5   2. I need to be noticed for how I look or act.

1 2 3 4 5   3. I need to be known for something special.

1 2 3 4 5   4. When I've done something great, I will make sure people find out.

1 2 3 4 5   5. Accomplishment without recognition is not fully rewarding.

SECTION 19

1 2 3 4 5   1. I need to feel safe from what is likely to happen.

1 2 3 4 5   2. I need to feel safe from what might (yet is unlikely) to happen.

1 2 3 4 5   3. I need to ensure people close to me are fully protected.

1 2 3 4 5   4. I feel uncomfortable starting something new and am unsure of any risks.

1 2 3 4 5   5. When I don't take every possible precaution, I feel uncomfortable.

SECTION 20

1 2 3 4 5   1. I need to perform a job or engage in regular work.

1 2 3 4 5   2. I need to keep busy with things.

1 2 3 4 5   3. I need to do even more than I am doing now.

1 2 3 4 5   4. When I am idle, I am nervous or uncomfortable.

1 2 3 4 5   5. When I am not working, I feel guilty.

PART TWO – RANK YOUR NEEDS

In Part Two, summarize the Needs Evaluation from Part One. First write the **total** score received for each Section (1-20) in the column. Next, circle the **5 lowest scores.** These are your most critical needs.

_____ Section 1: Acceptance

_____ Section 2: Accomplishment

_____ Section 3: Acknowledgements/Compliments

_____ Section 4: Be Loved

_____ Section 5: Be Right

_____ Section 6: Cared For

_____ Section 7: Certainty/Clarity/Accuracy

_____ Section 8: Comfort

_____ Section 9: Communication

_____ Section 10: Control/Dominate

_____ Section 11: Critical Link/Be Needed

_____ Section 12: Duty/Obligation

_____ Section 13: Freedom

_____ Section 14: Honesty/Integrity

_____ Section 15: Order/Perfection

_____ Section 16: Peace/Quietness

_____ Section 17: Power

_____ Section 18: Recognition

_____ Section 19: Safety/Security

_____ Section 20: Work

My Critical Needs:

1. _____

2. _____

3. _____

4. _____

5. _____

PART THREE – GO DEEPER – YOUR EXACT NEED

In Part Three, go to each of your Critical Needs and circle the word that best describes the "Exact Need" within each "Area of Need".

AREA OF NEED	EXACT NEED	AREA OF NEED	EXACT NEED
1. Accepted	Approved of	**11. Be Needed**	Critical Link
	Be Included		Useful
	Be Permitted		Important
	Respected		Be Material
2. Accomplish	Achieve	**12. Duty**	Obligated
	Fulfill		Follow
	Finish		Do Right/Good
	Realize		Have a Task
3. Acknowledged	Complimented	**13. Freedom**	Unrestricted
	Appreciated		Privileged
	Admired		Immune
	Valued		Independent
4. Be Loved	Liked	**14. Honesty**	Uprightness
	Cherished		Openness
	Esteemed		Frankness
	Held Fondly		Integrity
5. Be Right	Morally Correct	**15. Order**	Perfection
	Not Mistaken		Placement
	True		Harmony
			Rightness
6. Be Cared For	Attention	**16. Peace**	Quietness
	Concerned		Stillness
	Helpful		Serenity
	Cared For		Balance
7. Certainty	Clarity	**17. Power**	Authority
	Accuracy		Capacity
	Assurance		Omnipotence
	Obviousness		Vigour
8. Comfort	Luxury	**18. Recognition**	Be Noticed
	Ease		Remembered
	Contented		Known for
	Leisure		Regarded Well
9. Communicate	Be Heard	**19. Safety**	Secure
	Speak		Protected
	Share		Stable
	Inform		Known
10. Control	Dominate	**20. Work**	Perform
	Command		Labour
	Restrain		Industrious
	Manage		Busy

Now that you know your Critical Needs and your Exact Need in each of the areas, transfer them to a sticky note or colourful note card and keep them somewhere handy so that you can easily remember them.

By knowing and honouring your needs, you will find more ease in your life.

Honouring Your Needs

You have identified your needs, and now you must honour them. Let's evaluate whether you are applying this information to ensure you are taking care of yourself.

If your needs are not being met, what happens? How do you feel? How do you behave? We may be able to compromise and not have one or more of our needs met in the short term. However, over time, the more we put others' needs ahead of our own, the more off balance we become; eventually, resentment and negativity grow. This leads to negative behaviours and keeps us in those lower vibrational states that hold us back from attracting the successful outcomes we desire. There are certain cues that you are not honouring your own needs — anxiety, depression, a lack of fulfilment, or general crankiness are definite symptoms of not having your needs met.

We are typically looking forward. What is on our list of things to do today? What steps do we need to take to achieve our goals? We march forward and focus on forces outside of ourselves to achieve outcomes. We get some results and make some progress. But it often comes at the expense of feeling overwhelmed or exhausted. Without honouring our internal needs and taking care of ourselves first, we quickly run out of motivation and the energy to elevate our potential. Therefore, the goal is to take care of ourselves first — fuel our own tanks, charge our own batteries, meet our own needs — so we can then move forward and serve at the next level.

Connecting Deeper

There is one more extremely powerful exercise you can do to get a pulse for what you need the most in any given moment, week, year, or season. Within each of us lies the most pure and whole versions of ourselves — our soul or higher selves. You may have also heard of this divine part of you referred to as your "little girl" or "little boy" self. You can check in anytime with this part of yourself to see what you need. The more you check in, the more comfortable you will feel using this tool; however, if this is new to you, then expect that it may feel different, like all new things.

In order to check in with this part of yourself, I recommend doing the following exercise to become acquainted with your "little self".

First, find a quiet space where you will not be interrupted, and you can get comfortable. If you can light a candle, this will help support you during this process. Sit with your back straight and your legs crossed or in any other position that feels the most comfortable for you. If sitting in a chair with your feet on the ground feels best, go with that. Make sure the temperature of the room feels right, and if wrapping yourself in a blanket feels good, go ahead and do that.

Sit quietly, close your eyes, and make this declaration either out loud or silently to yourself, "I would like to meet my little self." Then, just be. Imagine yourself walking down a path that opens into a field. Your little self will meet you here. Let whatever images come into your mind arise. You will be met with images of yourself before the age of seven. Imagine interacting with this child. How do they look? Are they happy, sad, or afraid? Spend some time with them. Ask them what they need. Do what feels natural, whether that is picking them up, hugging them, or reassuring them that everything will be okay. Once you feel like you have had enough time with them, let them know that they are not alone and that you will always protect them and make sure they are well cared for and nurtured. Let them know how much they truly matter. Then say goodbye for now, walk back up the path, open your eyes, and return to the present day.

The first time I did this exercise was highly emotional for me. When I connected with Little Girl Diane, she appeared as the version of me just after losing my sister. She was small and vulnerable and alone. She had cute lop-sided ponytails and a pure heart. I remember sobbing as I collected her in my lap, hugged her, and told her she was not alone. I felt like she had been left alone in this void space for a very long time. This moment of reconnecting with her and giving her the care and attention she always deserved was a breakthrough moment.

Another time, I did this exercise when I was deep in the suffering of a relationship. My needs were not being met, and things were not going in the direction I desired. However, I was holding on, hoping and believing that things would change and move forward because I so desperately wanted to create my "happily ever after" with my partner. After months of conflict, I was feeling upset, so I decided to connect with my little self. When I became quiet and made my intention, I could see my

little self crouched down in a corner trying to protect herself.
She was trembling and afraid. In that moment, I knew things
had to change. When I collected her and rocked her back and
forth, I promised her that I would never put her in that situa-
tion again. I would love her first and take care of her needs so
that she could feel happy, protected, and loved.

When we look in the mirror and see the current adult versions of ourselves, most times we have a lot of judgement or expectation. We might think we are intelligent and capable beings and should be doing a lot more. But if we look deeper, beyond the reflection, there is a human soul that has needs, desires, unhealed wounds, and triggers; we are simply trying to do our very best in this ever-challenging experience we call life. If you can connect to a deeper part of yourself and give yourself the real self-care and nurturing you need, you can make a monumental shift in your being that will boost your level of consciousness and allow you to lift off to a new level of success, happiness, and abundance.

Defining and Communicating Boundaries

You now have a deeper understanding of your needs, so it is much easier to identify what boundaries you might wish to establish. When you consider your boundaries in a proactive way, it allows you to be clearer and kinder when communicating them. Practising this in advance will enable you to build confidence in advocating for yourself. This will also shift you away from seeing boundaries as those big, bad grey walls that are there to protect you from people trying to take advantage of you. This is important as when we imagine our boundaries like this, it results in our communication coming across as harsh or abrupt. When you embrace boundaries as positive, protective guidelines that are necessary to ensure you are being respected, this self-love and kindness will translate into a well-communicated, non-abrasive message.

Let's take some time now to intentionally work through defining some of your work and personal boundaries and proactively plan a kind, yet direct way to communicate them in the event that they are a future requirement.

Work Boundaries

1. When it comes to work, what do you need to ensure your needs are being met?

2. What boundaries do you have or need to have in your work life?

3. Why are these important?

4. What happens if you do not respect these boundaries?

5. Can you think of a time at work in the last six months where you felt unhappy because you extended beyond what felt comfortable, or you did something out of fear that if you did not, you would lose respect or an opportunity?

6. Are there any other boundaries you would now like to add to your work boundaries?

Now, pick one of your boundaries and imagine a supervisor or colleague asking you to extend beyond this boundary. Think of how communicating your boundary in a defensive versus non-defensive way would sound. Write these two options down so that when you are faced with having to exercise a boundary, you will feel more prepared and come across in a positive way. This will support you in feeling much more confident and in being perceived in a positive way — a key ingredient to success.

Here is an example:

Your boss tells you this project is critical, and you are going to have to work extra hours over the coming weeks to help the team get it done.

Defensive Boundary Setting Communication: I am not available to work extra time. I work really hard as it is. You don't pay me enough to do anything more.

Positive Boundary Setting Communication: I understand this project is very important to our team, and I am very committed to doing my best work to help in achieving a successful outcome; however, I am not always available to work additional hours due to my other commitments. You can count on me to be highly focused and to get my work done within my regular hours.

Word choice and tone matter. By thinking through and writing down your responses in advance, you will feel prepared when having to exercise and communicate boundaries.

Now, let's move on to your personal life.

Personal Life Boundaries

1. When it comes to your personal life, what do you need to ensure your needs are being met?

2. What boundaries do you have or need to have with your partner, children, extended family, and friends?

3. Why are these important?

4. What happens if you do not respect these boundaries?

5. Can you think of a time in your personal life in the last six months where you felt unhappy because you extended beyond what felt comfortable, or you did something out of fear that if you did not, you would lose respect or an opportunity?

6. Are there any other boundaries you would now like to add to your personal life boundaries?

Now, pick one of your boundaries and imagine a friend, relative, or your partner asking you to extend beyond your boundary. Think of how communicating your boundary in a defensive versus non-defensive way would sound. Write these two options down so that when you have to exercise this boundary, you will feel more prepared and come across in a positive way. This will support you by building your confidence and making you feel more comfortable in your communication.

Here is an example:

Your mother-in-law wants you to come for Christmas dinner at her house every year on Christmas Day.

Defensive Boundary Setting Communication: Why do you expect us to do that? That is so inconsiderate, and it's never going to happen.

Positive Boundary Setting Communication: Mom, we really appreciate how much Christmas means to you and how much you love us and want us to be a part of that. However, it's just not possible. We have decided what works best for us is to rotate, so we will spend Christmas Day with you every third year. Of course, we will celebrate the holidays with you each year to have that family connection. We will work in advance to schedule a day that works well for all of us.

If you have struggled to define and communicate boundaries, understand that it is completely normal. In fact, it likely means that you are a very kind and generous person. The only problem is that without boundaries, resentment and tension will build, eventually bubbling over into either an internal or external blowup.

Defining and positively communicating your boundaries when necessary is a proactive self-care strategy that will allow you to have your needs met and feel more balanced. This supports your ability to show up as a kind and highly valued person who emits a high-vibration energy that attracts the life you most desire.

CHAPTER 13
Lift Off

"You will never have a greater or lesser dominion than that over yourself. The height of a person's success is gauged by their self-mastery, the depth of their failure by their self-abandonment. They who cannot establish dominion over themselves will not have dominion over others."
Leonardo da Vinci

The path of elevating your consciousness to create more success and abundance is a lifetime process. However, once you understand the real reason you feel held back and unfulfilled, you can take intentional steps to start moving forward. When you commit to yourself and doing the internal work, you will notice positive changes and understand how truly powerful you are.

Becoming a conscious leader begins with looking inwards and serving yourself. When you serve yourself by letting go of that which is no longer useful to you, processing your stagnant emotions, and healing the root causes of your imbalance, you can shed heavy layers of energy that are holding you back from feeling truly happy, fully engaged in life, and deeply fulfilled.

This is the secret sauce to what will lead you to the success you desire.

Once you begin practicing self-mastery, you are intentionally choosing to lead yourself to the successful, happy life your soul desires. By releasing and healing wounds and emotions that are causing triggered, undesirable behaviours, you are creating space for a new identity. This allows you to create a crystal-clear vision, shift your stories, and ensure you are aways moving from the space of victim to victor. Once you have achieved a balanced and whole state of well-being, you can then spring forward to a place of healthy service to others, to positive and rewarding servant leadership.

We struggle so much to create balance in our lives because we constantly seek answers outside of ourselves when everything we need to understand or shift lies within us.

We have been conditioned to believe that taking care of ourselves is selfish. We value being generous and serving others, which is highly valuable, but only if we are first serving and being generous to ourselves. Failure to do so only leads to imbalance and a low energetic frequency. When we serve from that unhealed or unbalanced place, we typically do so because we are seeking something in exchange — validation, affirmation, or love. When we are in this cycle of serving to receive something in exchange, it is usually to fill a void within us.

However, as we find out, no amount of external praise or recognition does actually fill the void. Often, we continue to give, give, give and hope that the external validation will fill up that void within us, but it never does. That void can only be filled by going inwards and healing the root cause of what created the void in the first place. Eventually, continuing to be generous from this unhealthy space will only lead to resentment.

This unhealthy generosity results in two outcomes. First, the resentment leads to negative behaviours like passive-aggressiveness or needy comments or outbursts; this certainly does not help the way you are perceived by others and definitely affects your path to creating successful outcomes. Secondly, the feelings of resentment affect your state of ease, moving you to a place of dis-ease in your body, having a negative impact on your cells, and ultimately creating physical disease.

Have you ever seen the work of Dr. Masuro Emoto, a Japanese researcher, called *The Hidden Messages in Water*? Dr. Emoto took photographs of frozen crystals of water in different bottles and labelled them with different words. The images illustrate the power of our thoughts and feelings on water. High-vibration, positive words like "love" or "thank you" crystalized into beautiful images, whereas low-vibration, negative words like "hate" or "kill" crystalized into unbalanced, ugly, and disturbing crystal images. If you consider that humans are roughly 60% water and that your internal voice is always speaking to you (resulting in an emotional response), it is easy to see how much power your thoughts and feelings have over your cellular function and the physical responses in your body. Therefore, it is imperative that your mental, emotional, and spiritual realms are in a balanced place to ensure you are informing a strong and healthy body that can serve from a place of wellness.

In the desperate pursuit of work-life balance, a lot of buzz has surrounded self-care. Unfortunately, most of it is surface-level fluff. Yes, of course, it feels nice to take a bubble bath or treat yourself to a spa day — it may also be a treat for your parasympathetic nervous system. But true self-care needs to go deeper if it is to actually yield meaningful results. It entails putting yourself first each and every day. Failure to do so will only leave you in an unhealthy cycle of serving from an empty cup and eventually feeling resentful.

However, when you focus on real self-care and doing the work that makes a difference, you move into a space of wholeness. You begin to show up differently and people appreciate, recognize, or thank you. These kind gestures no longer go towards filling a void but can truly be received; the rewarding feeling only enhances that high-vibrational state where success flows towards you with ease.

In order to truly be a conscious leader, you must first know how to lead yourself. This involves deepening your self-awareness and consciously healing patterns that result from the unhealed or shadow parts of yourself.

These patterns are the real obstacle to what is holding you back and preventing you from living in a natural state of ease, enlightenment, and abundant success.

For centuries, we have been informed by our societal practices that create structures, limits, and ideas that keep us safe. There is a great sense of fear that without this order, there will be chaos. We have outsourced a great deal of our power and authority. We trust in our governments and industries to inform us and provide us with valuable information that will serve our best interests.

And yet — something just doesn't feel right.

Something is missing. You know you have the intelligence and talent to experience more success, balance, and fulfilment and yet you are somehow craving more. You know it's out there. You can feel it, just off in the distance. You just don't quite know how to achieve it. But you do now. The answers are within you.

Everything you need to know to have the career and the personal life you desire is within you.

You and only you have the power to create the life you desire — the vital, strong healthy body, the sharp, relaxed, calm mind, the peaceful, open, full heart, and the expansive, connected and lit-up spirit. Stop giving your power away. Stop looking for others to save you or make you happy. Use structures and organizations to support you and advise you, but never to decide for you. The power to create healthy balance, to elevate your potential, to be successful ... is within you.

We have been programmed to look for and point to factors outside of ourselves for why we are not thriving. This life experience is not for the faint of heart; life is hard! However, giving our power away to external factors that lie outside of our circle of influence only places us in a low-vibration state of victimhood. When we come back within and focus on how we can heal the things that are holding us back, we take our authority back. We let go of our heavy burdens and the ties that are holding us back — we are able to lift off, rising above the crowd with ease.

Success and abundance are your birthright. Everything you desire is possible because you are a champion! I believe in you! By reading this book and doing the exercises in it, I know that you will rise above the crowd, level up, and shine brighter than ever before.

You've got this!

Acknowledgements

This book certainly did not come together without the knowledge, support, wisdom, and love of many. First, to my clients. I have learned so much from you and in many cases, you have become my friends and extended family. Supporting you and seeing you thrive brings so much joy to my life. Thank you for trusting me and allowing me to be on your "Board of Directors". To Megan Williams and the team at The Self Publishing Agency (TSPA) — you guys are total ROCK STARS and have guided and supported me through this process. Thank you, Ira, Andrea, Petya, and Tage. To Erik at Insightful Automations, thank you for your technical brilliance. To my bestie, Ana, who has listened to every single thought at every single stage of this book, believed in me, and cheered me on — your constant support and unconditional love truly make me a better human. To my amazing mom who made me a second-generation author, your strength, courage, and grace is my guiding light. Words alone cannot express how much admiration and love I have for you. To my dad, who left us too soon but still serves as my north star. Your legacy of success and kindness is something I strive to emulate each and every day. You are my leadership role model and forever hero. To my incredible children, Ally and Matthew. You are my proudest accomplishment and my reason to reach for the stars. It is my deepest desire that I build a legacy that you will be proud of — just as proud as I am of both of you. I must also acknowledge my sister, Laurie. Although her soul chose to stay for a short time in this lifetime, her impact and continued connection to me has been instrumental in my purpose and legacy. I know she was with me every page of this book. And lastly, but most importantly, to you, the reader — thank you for taking the time to invest in yourself. Your dreams matter. Remember ... success is your birthright. I believe in you. You've got this!

About the Author

Diane Taylor is the Founder and Principal Consultant of Glow Leadership. She is a speaker, author, leadership development coach, and strategic human resources consultant with over thirty years of professional experience across several industries. Diane is passionate about helping others discover and ignite their highest potential in their careers and personal lives. She has spent her career developing a deep understanding of humans, the way they behave, and how to bring out the best in them. What sets Diane apart from other coaches is her deeply intuitive insight and empathy of others navigating the human experience. Through her own personal childhood tragedy, she learned the hard way how to take her power back and take care of her own well-being, enabling her to emerge a victor. It is her purpose and passion to hold a space for others attempting to overcome unprocessed emotion and the unhealed wounds that are ultimately holding them back from the life and success they truly desire.